LEGACY
—— OF A ——
SHARECROPPER'S
Daughter

QUEEN B. BRAILEY

LEGACY OF A SHARECROPPER'S DAUGHTER

Queen B. Brailey
ecconnectors@yahoo.com

ISBN: 978-1-943342-00-6

Printed in the United States of America.
First Edition

Book Cover Design: Leo Twiggs, PhD., International Artist
Supporter: Rosa Twiggs
Research and Pictures: Mrs. Linda Robertson

Design and Published by: Destined To Publish
www.DestinedToPublish.com

FOREWORD

Queen Brailey is among the many unsung heroes who have truly made the world a better place. She did not allow her childhood as a sharecropper's daughter to define her and she has not allowed that limited circumstance to contain her. To the contrary, those conditions seem to have provided her a strong will and foundation upon which to achieve and flourish.

I met Queen when we arrived as Freshmen on the campus of South Carolina State College (now University) SCSU, back in 1957. I learned quickly that this young woman from Fountain Inn, South Carolina would blaze a trail on campus and become a formidable force in society. She worked hard and was a much better student than I was, although that was not hard to achieve. I knew that her positive attitude would carry her far in life.

Upon graduation Queen dedicated her life to young people. Her career in early childhood education was born out of a desire to give every child an opportunity to excel. Her commitment and dedication to her profession and her own children, grandchildren and great-grandchildren were born out of love of family. And her ministry with mothers and daughters are rooted in her deep and abiding faith.

I am reading Sharecropper's Daughter during Women History Month and while commemorating the 56th anniversary of "Bloody Sunday, March 7, 1965. Reading this book and remembering the experiences I shared with Queen during the years we spent together on SCSU's campus - 1957 to 1961- are reminders of how far we have come, and how far we still have to go, in order to overcome the current effects of the socio-economic circumstances of our nation's past.

The Sharecropper's Daughter is the inspirational story of a life well lived and a dream realized. If it is true that success is not defined by great wealth or fancy titles, but by what you have done for others, Queen Brailey is one of the most successful women I know.

James E. "Jim" Clyburn, SC-6
United States Congress

DEDICATIONS

To my late Father and Mother, who are always in my heart.

My two daughters, Necole and Crystal, who inspired me to write the book.

My grandchildren, Jasmine, James, Jamauri, Aubrai, Whitney, Wynter, and Will, who express love for me like no one else can. My great-grands, Serenity, Kalia, and Shya, who hold the key to my heart.

My goddaughter Nathalina, who always keeps me in her prayers. My goddaughter Cynthia, who loves me beyond infinity.

My sisters and brothers, Lula, Hannah, Henrietta, Dorothy, Yvonne, Henry Jr., John Lewis, James Thomas, and Mentone, who provided fun times through hard times.

High school and college students who feel like the journey to success is too hard, keep going, God will see you through.

Young professionals in your first few years who may have thought about making changes but are afraid of being fired, just remember, when one door closes, God will open another.

Others who helped me along the way,
I love you.

ACCOLADES FOR THE QUEEN "B"

Queen B. Brailey's extraordinary record of initiatives and accomplishments gives testament to a lifestyle dedicated to helping others. She is a serious-minded individual who is highly motivated, self-directed, ambitious and committed to the concept of "improving the quality of life for individuals and families throughout the life cycle."

I have known Queen since her high school days as an athlete and student council officer. Throughout the years, relationships were fostered as undergraduates at SC State, and our paths later intersected as colleagues in the profession of Family and Consumer Sciences, through our involvement in community activities and during special celebrations.

Queen's many professional positions demonstrated evidence of outstanding human and materials resource management skills; creativity and ingenuity when addressing programmatic problems; and excellent personal relations skills, working effectively both independently and as a team member. Her orientation and leadership skills are also evident through the receipt of special recognition and numerous awards.

Queen's successful career and subsequent retirement are evidence of her valued contributions to society. I am honored to have known her over the years as a colleague and a friend.

Lillie Beasley Glover, PhD, CFCS
Professor Emeritus, SCSU

•••••••••••••••••••••••

To the Queen "B," what you have done in the 55 years I have known you has been amazing. You began as a cook at the preschool (now Child Development Learning Center) on the campus of South Carolina State College (now University) and rose to the rank of Assistant Professor and Teacher of the Year for the Department of Family and Consumer Sciences. Yes, I've known you as a cook, teacher assistant, teacher, instructor, co-worker, friend, and the best neighbor one could ever have. It was a joy working with you as a teacher and as the Director of South Carolina State University's Preschool. You always said, "I am not a boss but a member of the team."

You have been by my side through happy times as well as all my sorrows, the death of my son and my husband. I remember when my husband passed, you packed your clothes and came and stayed with me one week. You are loving, caring, kind, spiritual and my best friend.

Barbara Butler,
Best friend, neighbor, and co-worker

• •

Queen Brailey speaks with a strong voice for the many of her generation who have endured with extraordinary resiliency. Through Legacy of a Sharecropper's Daughter, her voice sheds light on a potential path forward as we struggle to navigate societal challenges of the new normal. The best way to tell where you're going is to understand where you've been.

State Representative
Jerry Govan

• •

It gives me pleasure and pride to share the feelings I have for my sister-in-law Queen Brailey on the publication of this book. Queen is a phenomenal God-fearing lady who I have known for over sixty years.

Over the years I have observed Queen's accomplishments leading her to become a pillar of support in the Orangeburg Community. As she lays out so nicely in her book, Queen has experienced an extraordinary, well-rounded life while demonstrating love and compassion for her fellow human beings. She has excelled as a wife, mother, grandmother, great-grandmother, aunt, educator, business proprietor, author, Christian advocate and friend.

She has been recognized and acknowledged for numerous achievements, including South Carolina House of Representatives resolutions and being named Outstanding Woman of the Year in 1974. From her various experiences noted in her book, it is evident that Queen's admiration for serving the church and children of the Orangeburg Community has been her greatest ambition. In summary, the "Sharecropper's Daughter" is a dynamic human being, and I am so fortunate to have her as my sister-in-law and friend. I hope you enjoy the benefits from reading The Legacy of a Sharecropper's Daughter, for this is a book of inspiration for dreamers.

Col. Ret. Jerry A Hubbard

•••••••••••••••••••••

Mother Queen, a gentle spirit whose kindness, character, charm, grace, humility, intelligence, compassion and love have touched the lives of countless children and adults throughout these United States and beyond through her commitment to authentic early education practices and principles. We are blessed beyond measure to learn more about our Queen Mother who has devoted her life to giving children and adults the tools to flourish. May her legacy forever inspire, motivate and encourage future generations to ensure the children are doing well.

Darnell Byrd Baptiste McPherson, LBSW
Executive Director, Darlington County First Steps

•••••••••••••••••••••

Mrs. Queen Brailey is without a shadow of doubt "Second to None!" She is a very seasoned and highly effective educator who I have known personally all my life.

My own children attended her Learning Center in Orangeburg, South Carolina, "Kids World." The continuous academic excellence of all children who went there (including my own) is proof that Mrs. Brailey knows her craft.

She studied under the leadership of renowned researcher David Weikart, who developed the highly effective, research-based curriculum model known as HighScope. This model is used all over the world now. Because I knew first hand the value of this wise lady, I solicited her professional expertise to work with teachers in my current public school district. She demands that the realities of everyday living that the children experience be included in the learning processes for teachers. While she always maintains an impeccably professional demeanor, it is no big deal to find her working on the floor with teachers. See ... she knows that they must personally get down into the learning modalities first to comprehend every aspect that it takes to create a conducive environment that meets children exactly where they learn.

If you don't know Mrs. Brailey, you would think that she was a quiet, soft spoken, little lady who was like an average person in a local town. BOY, IS THAT WRONG! They just don't make educators like her anymore. She explodes with every wonderful characteristic, and even more, that you can imagine in the best teacher for your child. Whenever I was around her, it was my desire to learn all that I could from her. It became blatantly obvious to me that children and teachers who cross her path are touched by a divinely appointed "Merchant of Hope" who, in the end, positively influences their lives in a way that would yield nothing but sincere love, truth, and greatness.

Carlita S. Davis
Assistant Superintendent
Office of Curriculum, Instruction, & Assessment

•••••••••••••••••••••••

Queen Esther Berry Brailey, you are known as one who loves children from early years even into adulthood. Your love is so great that you travel to teach Early Childhood all over the United States. With that background, God laid on your heart to write and publish a book, All Aboard the Unit Express, to help with the path that young teachers will encounter. Because of your love for children, it became embedded in your own children. Your daughters are now following in your own footsteps. The love in your heart is not just given in the public eye.

You have been a great support to your immediate and extended family by traveling several miles when needed. God has really blessed your heart with love. Every day your siblings look forward to hearing your voice by telephone. Your perseverance has caused many lives to change and be drawn to Christ through you. Continue to let your light shine before men, women, boys and girls that they may see your good works and glorify the heavenly Father. Queen, as I think about your life, God has brought you from the cotton fields to where you are today. It has been my privilege to travel this journey with you.

Dorothy Ann Berry Chapman Pearson
Sister and Best Friend

•••••••••••••••••••••••

To write about Queen Brailey as a friend and colleague is probably difficult in that there is so much to be said. You have to decide which are the most important things you want to say without writing an entire book yourself. Our story begins with me meeting Queen B., as she was sometimes referred to by Nick Brailey, her late husband.

My next encounter with Queen was as the Director of South Carolina's Training And Technical Assistance, Region IV Head Start Programs. South Carolina State University became the grantee for this program, funded through a grant from what was then the Department of Health, Education, and Welfare (HEW). The purpose of the grant was to provide training to teachers in this anti-poverty programs for disadvantaged children and parents from 0-6.

One of the reasons the grant was housed at this HBCU was that they had a strong early childhood program. HEW needed more Black institutions of higher learning involved, and ninety per cent of children enrolled in the program were black. In viewing Queen's background, the University felt she was the person for the program. One of the things I learned early was that if she had an idea, she was not going to let go until you convinced her that it was not going to work because of timing and regulations. Most things can be resolved if they can get beyond those two measures.

One of the things, among many, that I always admired about Queen was her enthusiasm for the people she worked with: parents, children and staff. To observe her working with either group always made me endeavor to be a better colleague and supervisor. Her ability to make children and adults feel better about themselves was one of the most transformational acts I have ever witnessed and in my estimation one of the most important weapons we as trainers could ever have in our arsenal.

To say that Queen is one of the best Early Childhood development trainers I have ever witnessed is probably an understatement. In all the years I have known her, she has never run out of ideas or energy. Your contributions to the early childhood community of South Carolina have been voluminous and worthy of recognition by the state, something I hope will happen while you can still enjoy it.

There are probably many things I would have said about you if this opportunity had come prior to my (90th) birthday. Just the same, I am glad I had the opportunity to describe my involvement in your long and productive career.

Queen Brailey has shared with us her vision of early childhood education with an understanding of how important parents are to that process and with a zeal that would put a Baptist Preacher to shame. As she marches into the sunset of her career, we wish her only the best of everything.

Edward Vaughn, Ret. Supervisor
Health, Education and Welfare
Region IV Head Start for North and
South Carolina, Kentucky & Tennessee

•••••••••••••••••••••

A random selection of which pew to sit on in church some twenty-five plus years ago ended up being a blessing for the Nimmons family. On that pew at Trinity United Methodist, we found a kind heart, wise counsel, a brave spirit, and bold faith all wrapped up in Queen B. Brailey. She's became our bonus mom/grandmom and has helped us celebrate our successes, held us during our trials and prayed for us daily. Ernest, Skyler and I love her dearly and truly know our lives have been enriched by her presence.

Ernest, Michelle, and Skyler Nimmons

•••••••••••••••••••••

Queen B. Brailey is a singular woman among women. A woman of great character and generosity, it has been one of my life's blessings to know her. She is a living treasure who deserves any and all accolades that could be bestowed upon her. She is the original Queen B.

Antonia Roberts, Friend

•••••••••••••••••••••••

Queen Brailey is my baby sister, and we had many adventures together growing up. When we played on the same basketball team, she was my favorite guard. We were very competitive. One night we played one of our rivals, Sterling High School. The game was very close, and my sister was amazing that night. She was tenacious and persistent, which allowed us to win the game. I have always seen those qualities in her since she was a little girl. TODAY she has accomplished a lot, and it is because of her persistence. I love you, Sis!

Your Sister,
Yvonne Berry Taylor

•••••••••••••••••••••••

My sister Queen has a kind heart and always concerned for her family. Whenever she came home for a visit she always came with gifts for all the young kids. She was sandwiched between the five girls and four boys. She is rather spoiled, however a good spoiled.

She always taught the younger kids about entrepreneurship. She asked us to save our money received from picking scrap cotton and make plans to use it. She is greatly loved by the 130 offspring of Henry and Lucille Berry

James Berry - Brother

•••••••••••••••••••••••

CONTENTS

Contents

INTRODUCTION

This book tells the story of me as a young girl, born a sharecropper's daughter in a family of ten children in a three-bedroom house. I tell of the pain experienced working long hours in the cotton and corn fields. There were many struggles as I balanced my education with working on the farm, missing days in school and doing homework by a kerosene lamp. However, maintaining high grades was a requirement of Daddy and Mom. It was a disappointment when it seemed that I would not be able to attend college due to lack of funds. It seemed as if the countless three-mile walks to school during the cold winter days and hot summer afternoons were in vain. However, my future was spared by a so-called homeless man who saved the day.

Segregation and the presence of the KKK began early in my life when the word "nigger" was used toward my father. His life was threatened with the promised of being lynched. However, there were also happy times when the family played games, went to high school and college graduations, and attended family reunions.

I tell of how God, a strong family, and the church have been the sources of my inspiration throughout my life. I believe this book will be an inspiration for high school students, college students, and future educators at a time when they feel the journey is too hard to continue. It also gives credence to the importance of standing up for justice and doing what is right.

CHAPTER ONE

The Setting

"The Inn"—The Original Fountain Inn.
FOUNTAIN INN. S. C.

"The Fountain."

*M*any years have passed since I gave thought to where my life began. It was in the red hills of Greenville County in South Carolina on McCarter Road. As I recall, the road was very curvy with lots of trees on both sides of the road and houses one to two miles apart. Our house was exactly three miles from Mt. Zion Baptist Church and Fountain Inn Elementary School in the little town of Fountain Inn, with the only transportation being that of two mules and a wagon or walking. I'm told the town was accidentally named after a gushing spring that resembled a fountain and an inn where the stagecoach drivers would stop to feed and water their livestock. The stagecoach drivers put the two together and began calling it Fountain Inn. The name caught on, and the town soon became Fountain Inn, population less than 6,000.

1

The house was built of wood with three bedrooms and a den/bedroom with a fireplace where Daddy and Mom slept. There was a kitchen with an eating area where family discussions took place and Daddy told stories about the Bible. Growing up, we shared beds, sometimes three to a bed. I believe that was one of the reasons we were so close as siblings. Lying there in bed, we shared all our little secrets. When one wanted to make a change in the bed, like turning over, we all had to agree.

The yard was free of grass. I am told the tradition of not growing grass in the yard came from Africa. We gathered twigs from an open field, tied them together in a bundle, and made a broom. It would take 30 to 50 minutes to sweep the yard clean because the brooms were rather small. When we finished, our backs would be very painful from bending over, but my daddy would say, "You don't have a back, only a gristle." If there was any grass left in the yard, even a sprig, we pulled it up.

There were very few conveniences. Our bathroom was on the outside; it was called an outhouse. Daddy and a neighbor would build the outhouse by digging a hole and building a small-looking closet over the hole. A wooden bench was built over the hole for individuals to sit on and hold personal hygiene. Personal hygiene supplies consisted of leaves, grass, ferns, and old magazines and sometimes toilet tissue. A lid was made to cover the hole to prevent mosquitoes and flies from breeding in the pit. The outhouse needed to be light enough that they could move it to a new hole before the year was over and cover the old one with dirt. It was a struggle to get out of the warm house in the wintertime to go outside in the rain, sleet, and sometimes snow to use the toilet.

During the night, we were allowed to use the potty. Early the next morning, depending on whose turn is was one of us would empty the potty in the outhouse.

There was a barn with a large fence around it that housed the livestock. The barn had a loft where the hay, which the livestock ate, was kept. The fence was poorly built, and many times the mules would get out and we would run after them until we corralled them back into the fixed fence. Sometimes neighbors would help, depending on how far the mules ran.

CHAPTER TWO

The Family

The boys: John Lewis, Henry Jr., Mentone, and James Thomas.
The girls: Hannah, Yvonne, Queen, Henry (the father) and Lucille (the mother),
Lula, Henrietta, and Dorothy.

My daddy and mom birthed thirteen children, six girls and seven boys. Three of the boys died at birth. I was at the end of the girls and the beginning of the boys. I was told the surrounding neighborhood

4

teased them because they had six girls, and everyone thought they were trying to have a boy. However, when the first boy came, they just enjoyed having more boys. They said it was true love.

Daddy was a strong, handsome man, about five feet six inches tall, with a fair complexion. He was born out of wedlock (his parents were not married), and it was known his father was a white man. He was given away at birth to a couple named Jim and Mammy (don't remember her first name) Berry. Daddy was a very happy man, always telling jokes. When he told jokes, he laughed louder than the people hearing the jokes. On a clear day, you could hear his laughter about a mile away. At age 16, Daddy found his only sister. Her name was Queen Esther, the name my Daddy gave me.

He also played jokes on his children and his wife. One day, my sister Yvonne and I were playing in the yard. Daddy came up and asked my sister to hold out her hand, then placed a caterpillar in it, knowing she was afraid. She almost fainted. Mom told Daddy never to do that again – she was very protective of her girls. I also recall one day, Mom was kneading (pounding) dough for her favorite buttermilk biscuits when Daddy began tickling her, and she slapped him upside the head with the dough. He said that was just love. His favorite word was HOT-TOE-MO-TIE .

My mom was a beautiful lady, five feet three inches tall and weighing roughly 130 lbs. She had long black hair and kept it in braids except for special occasions. She met Daddy at one of his baseball games. I'm told that when he saw her, he could not keep his eyes off of her. He lost the game but met the love of his life, and shortly afterward they were married.

Lucille, as my daddy affectionately called her, was a wonderful mother and wife, rather quiet in nature, but like a roaring lion when it came to her children. She controlled my daddy by saying, "Henry! That's enough, no more whipping." She was basically perfect, except when it came to fixing our hair. She had no skills in that department. It was a blessing when my older sisters learned how to give the younger ones beautiful hair styles. I think they knew something about Madam CJ Walker and the straightening comb. They would use the straightening comb to press our hair out. Afterward, they would take brown paper bags, cut them into strips, twist them, and roll our hair on them. They made the prettiest curls and could be used multiple times.

Daddy and Mom loved righteousness and hated weakness. We feel God anointed them with oil of gladness that kept them strong and capable of caring for their family (Psalm 45:7).

Mr. and Mrs. Henry Berry

A Portrait Of Family Fruitfulness

CHAPTER THREE

Experiences on the Farm

One day, a white man came to our house telling my Daddy what he wanted him to do and how soon he wanted it done. Listening from behind the big oak tree, I was able to hear the conversation. When the white man left, I asked Daddy who that white man thought he was talking to him that way. My Daddy turned to me and said, "Child, that man owns our house, the land, and most of the livestock. WE ARE SHARECROPPERS."

That was the first time I heard the word "sharecroppers." I asked Daddy to explain. He said, "Short Stuff" – that was the nickname Daddy gave me – "a sharecropper is a person who farms land for the owner in return for half the crop." I wanted to know why he would get half of the crop when he had done no work. We did all the work, sometimes from sunup to sundown, Sadly, Daddy said, "Because he owns it and we don't." A real disappointing reality check. Daddy and Mom would borrow money from the owner on a monthly basis to buy groceries and farming supplies. Very little was left except to buy a pair of shoes for the child who needed them the most.

Farming consisted of cotton, corn, wheat, sweet potatoes, white potatoes, a large garden with tomatoes, string beans, squash, watermelon, cantaloupe, peanuts, and sometimes strawberries. There were lots of pigs, cows, and chickens. Food was plentiful. During the summer and fall months, we did lots of canning. This is the process by which bacteria is removed from the food to preserve it for long periods of time. Mom, along with me and the other girls, canned foods such as tomatoes, string beans, peas, okra, corn, and pork sausages.

There was always an ample supply of milk, butter, and buttermilk. We would milk the cows, place some of the milk in a churn, cover it tightly, and when a white substance (clobber) formed on top of the milk, we would take the handle and churn up and down until butter was formed.

After the butter was removed, the leftover was buttermilk. The milk not placed in the churn was called sweet milk. It was used for drinking, especially for breakfast, and serving over grits and oatmeal. Many days when we came home from school, Mom had cooked cornbread. We would crumble the cornbread in a bowl and pour buttermilk over it. That was our meal before going into the field to work. I continue to eat cornbread and buttermilk today.

Eggs were plentiful, the main meal for breakfast. Along with scrambled eggs, we had hot biscuits, bacon, or sausage. Other mornings, we had hot biscuits with syrup. So, you see, we ate good on the farm.

To supplement the vegetable diet, Daddy would go rabbit and turtle hunting to get extra meat. He would sit under the big oak tree, with children watching, and clean the animals. It was said that the turtle meat represented all of the other meats we ate, such as chicken, fish, and pork chops. The meat was preserved by wrapping it in a piece of thin cloth and placing it in an ice box.

There was no electricity, so the ice was also wrapped in the thin cloth and placed in the top of the ice box to keep the food cool. The ice was delivered to our house once a week, and it usually lasted about a week. The only reason we got ice delivered was because my uncle drove the ice truck. The ice kept the bacteria from forming in the meat.

Chickens were available year-round, and when we wanted a chicken to eat, Daddy would say, "Come on, children, let's catch our dinner," and the race was on. Once we caught the chicken, Daddy would take it by the neck and swing it round and round until the neck popped. He would then remove the neck from the body and place the chicken in hot boiling water to loosen the feathers. It was the children's job to pick all the feathers off. Mom would sometimes make soup from the chicken feet. She said it replaced collagen and was good for colds and anything else that seemed to make you feel under the weather, so to speak.

The most exciting day on the farm was butchering the hogs. Butchering is the process of killing hogs so we would have meat during the winter and spring months. Daddy would invite a few of his masonic friends over to assist him. What they did first was put on three tin barrels of water and wait until it was boiling, and then they would kill the hog by piercing it in its neck. Once the hog was dead, they would dip it in hot water, then place it on a table to loosen the hair and scrape it off. Afterward, the hog was hung by rafters so they could cut it down the middle and remove the inside. It was the children, with the supervision of Mom, who separated the parts. This was the most horrible thing I ever had to do, except clean the chitterlings. Chitterlings are the intestines of the hog. This was not cool at all. However, today, some people view chitterlings as delicacies.

The hog was placed back on the table, and Daddy and his team would cut the meat from the skin into pork chops, bacon, roasts, and ribs. To preserve the meat, they would rub it with lots of salt and place it in an insulated box and close it tightly. Daddy said that was to draw the moisture out so the meat would last longer. I don't know where they got their scientific knowledge from. In the meantime, Mom would put the skin in the black pot and cook the grease out. The grease was used to make her buttermilk biscuits, bake cakes, fry meats, etc. We enjoyed eating the crisp skins. I guess you could say we ate high on the hog.

Mom was an excellent cook. She cooked three meals a day, breakfast, lunch, and dinner. She would say, "Children, wash your hands, come to the table and wait for your Daddy to say grace." We were taught table manners and to respect each other. We were a very close-knit family. After dinner, we would go outside to play. It would be dusk dark, and Mom and Daddy would sit on the porch. We caught lightning bugs (bugs that light up at night) and played games like hide and seek, hop scotch, jump rope, and playing with marbles. There were very few books, except school books and books from the school library. Daddy always read the Bible to us.

At the end of harvest season, Daddy and Mom would tell us they were going to THE BIG HOUSE, where the owner of the property lived, to settle up. Sometimes they went with their heads hanging low, especially if it was a bad year for crops, such as floods, lots of rain, or boll weevils. Boll weevils were little animals that got into the crops and would eat most of it. Sometimes spraying helped, but that cost money, and we had very little. When this happened, the debt was carried over to the next year, so we seldom were debt free. However, when there was a good year, Daddy and Mom would pay their debt and come home smiling. They would always bring two big packages of vanilla sandwich cookies, a jar of Duke's mayonnaise, bologna, and two loaves of bread to make sandwiches for celebrating. Oh, yes – can't forget a Pepsi-Cola for everyone.

Another downside of being a sharecropper was waiting for the owner to make repairs to the house, especially during the winter months. Sometimes we would wait months before he fixed leaks in the roof or replaced broken steps, front and back. Mom would take old blankets and coats and stuff them in the windows to keep the rain, sleet, snow, and wind from coming into the house. The summers were very hot, no electricity, only hand fans. Living in the deep country, we would always get a cool breeze at night by opening the windows. No worry of break-ins, because they knew the only thing they were able to steal was the love we had for each other, and that definitely was not for stealing.

CHAPTER FOUR

Elementary School

Queen B. age 10

*E*lementary school was a real challenge, having to walk three miles to school. Schools were segregated and buses were available for whites only. Mom would get up around five o'clock in the morning to prepare breakfast and fix lunches for us to take to school. Daddy would get ready to walk us through the woods, taking a shortcut. He placed a log across a creek and would hold our hands until we were safely across to the other side. Our parents were strong disciplinarians, but they had a love that could overpower any obstacles. We never thought of ourselves as being poor, because Daddy and Mom would always say that the most important thing in life is LOVE, and that came straight from God. I often wonder where they got so much knowledge in how to raise children when they only finished ninth grade. I guess when you believe in God, everything comes naturally.

Walking to school during the winter months was very hard. By the time we got to school, our hands and feet were freezing. However, our beloved teachers would place our hands and feet in warm water for a short period of time and dry them off with warm towels. The teachers said we could not learn if we were not comfortable. Our teachers were great, loving, and kind. Despite the obstacles, we kept our grades up and stayed on the honor roll. Sometimes it was hard to complete homework with five or six children trying to get close enough to see by the kerosene lamp, but we would always work it out, because Daddy and Mom would take no excuses.

Our teachers were like our second Mom and Daddy. We loved them and they loved us. Every morning we were required to recite a Bible verse. My favorite was the 23rd Psalm, because I learned that in Sunday School. (And now all parts of the Bible have been taken out of the schools – what a shame.) I don't think I understood the meaning of the 23rd Psalm then, but as I look back, I know that psalm has been a part of my life. The Lord has truly been my shepherd, leading me every day of my life. And when trouble came, God carried me through the most painful days of my life. Sometimes I believe there was only one set of footprints.

During harvest time, we missed many days of school because we were needed on the farm. Our teachers said we were smart kids and they did not want us to fall behind in our school work, so they would give us homework to review and complete. The teachers explained to Daddy how important school was and encouraged him to allow us to come to school at least three days a week. His reply was, "We have to work the crops in order to pay our debt."

I remember how we would tell time when we were in the cotton field. If you would stand straight up and your shadow was even with your body, it was 12:00. We would take off our sacks and tell Daddy it was time for lunch. It's an old wives' tale, but you should try it. I made sure I put this tale in my first book, All Aboard The Unit Express. This was one activity children really loved. On a sunny day, take children outside and have them stand up straight and hold a clock so they can make a comparison. A down-to-earth activity, so to speak. I also remember the large stinging worms that would sometime be hidden under the cotton leaves, though I don't remember what they were called. Sometimes we spent more time trying to see if worms were under the leaves than picking cotton, because their sting lasted for a long time and it really hurt.

When it rained and was too wet to harvest the crops, we were able to go to school, and in the afternoon, Daddy would play softball with us. Mom was the cheerleader for the girls. However, she spent most of that time making dresses for her girls using flour sacks. These were sacks Daddy got when he carried wheat to the mill to be thirsted into flour. The flour was then put into beautiful sacks, and without electricity, Mom used a pedal machine to make the dresses.

A wives' tale my Mom used to tell was that when you could hear the train loud and clear (we could hear it even out in the country), that was a sign it was going to rain. Ordinarily, we never heard the train. I think it had something to do with the acoustics in the air. I don't even know if she knew the word "acoustics," but believe it or not, Daddy and Mom knew a lot about science.

Laundry days were quite interesting. Three tin tubs and a black wash pot were set up outside. Once the clothes were wet in the first wash, they were then placed in the black pot to boil, and a stick was used to punch the clothes up and down to get the dirt out. (I am not sure now if that really got the dirt out.) Afterward, they were placed back in the second tub to be washed, and then the third tub to rinse the soap out.

Later, I learned how to make clothes look brighter and prettier by using homemade starch. The recipe Mom gave me was to use one to two gallons of water, bring it to a boil, mix together one half cup of flour to one cup of water, add to the boiling water, and allow to boil until it became smooth. There was no set recipe, so sometimes we had to add a little more water. When it was cool enough, we would put the clothes into the starch, wring them out, and hang them up to dry. They would be very stiff. Once the clothes were dry, I would sprinkle each piece with water, just enough to dampen them, wrap them in a dry cloth, and let them stand for at least half an hour.

In the meantime, I would heat the iron on the stove and iron the clothes. We looked really pretty when we went out. No one really knew they were flour sacks, because Mom added her special touch.

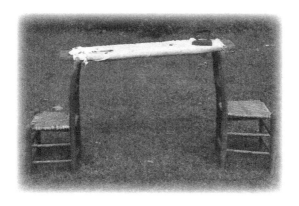

CHAPTER FIVE

High School

Henry Jr. kneeling, mom on the left daddy on the right. Back row from left to right
(Yvonne, Dorothy, Hannah, Henrietta and Me (Queen)

*H*igh school was great. We had so many activities to choose from, and it was the beginning of riding the school bus. We were also introduced to a party line telephone. A party line meant that everyone on McCarter Road was on the same line. So, if you picked up the phone to make a call and you heard a voice, you were supposed to hang the phone up.

However, knowing how curious people were, they would listen on the phone. They would find out other folks' business and begin to spread it.

Farming seemed to change, and Mom convinced Daddy to let us go to school more often. He began farming less land, plus three of the girls married and moved from the house. Sometimes Daddy would make a deal with other sharecroppers to work each other's farms, maybe two days at one farm and two days at the other. Many afternoons, my sister Yvonne and I stayed to practice basketball. We excelled in the game. On the days we had away games, the Home Economics teacher and the girls on the team would prepare food to eat before we left. People came from surrounding areas to see the Berry girls play. After all, we were very pretty, *really*, with a body to wish for and big, pretty legs. I suppose that came from the hard work on the farm.

I remember we were playing in a tournament, and the basketball coach sent a male student teacher to pick my sister and me up to go to the game. When we got up to leave, Daddy stepped in front of us and looked at the student teacher and said, "Where is the lady teacher?" The fellow said, "No one else was available." "Then you go back and get a female teacher," Daddy said. "I don't know you nor trust you." My sister and I cried, "Daddy, we're going to be late and we're playing for the championship!" His reply was, "No one will take advantage of my girls." The fellow went back and came back with a lady teacher. When we arrived, the game was in the first quarter and we were eight points behind. When we walked on the court, we received a standing ovation, and we won the game.

Queen first player standing from left next to Coach

I became so popular, I thought I could do almost anything. At one of our away games, I convinced the girls' and boys' basketball players to break the rule that said boys had to sit on one side of the bus and girls on the other side. This was in protest of our leaders, male and female teachers, sitting together. So, after the game, each boy sat on a seat with a girl. When the coach noticed, he told us to obey the rule, boys on one side and girls on the other side. Everyone moved except me, and the coach made me let the boy out. After all, it was my idea. The next day, Mr. Anderson, the principal, informed me that I would be expelled from school if I did not apologize to the student body. I refused and was expelled.

I played hooky from school for the next few days, pretending I was sick. After the third day, I looked out the window and saw my chemistry teacher, Mr. Pendarvis, whom I highly respected. I ran out of the house, down across the field, and hid behind the outhouse. My teacher told Daddy what had happened, and Daddy called me back and said if I did not come, he would come with a stick. I was surprised when Daddy agreed with me and said the teachers should set good examples. However, he said, "You broke the rules, and you must apologize." That taught me a real lesson in justice, that no one is above the law.

I became very active in other school and church organizations and represented them at local, county, and state events. It was good for me – my high school principal and Sunday school teacher said it would help me stay out of trouble. I began to change my self-centered ways and understand that rules, even if I did not agree with them, must be followed until they were legally changed. I began reading the Bible and gaining an understanding that there were rules we all must live by, the Ten Commandments, and there was someone greater than Daddy and Mom, *GOD!*

The thing about God is that he is always there when you need him. For instance, one Saturday, Mom, my sisters, and I were sitting on the front porch when a white man, who appeared to be drunk, stumbled into the yard and began calling us the "B" word. Just at that time, Daddy drove up in the wagon returning from getting supplies for the week. He asked the white man kindly to leave the yard, but the man refused and continued cursing. Daddy picked him up, threw him in the wagon, and started down the road toward Fountain Inn. Mom ran behind the wagon yelling, "Henry, don't kill him, Henry, please don't kill him!" A short while later, Daddy returned with blood on his clothing. Mom asked in a very soft voice, "Henry, did you kill him?" Daddy said, "No, but he won't come in this yard again."

Daddy got word that the Ku Klux Klan (KKK) was coming to lynch him. He carried Mom and the children to Grandma Hannah's house, contacted his masonic brothers, and told them what was going to happen. They came with shot guns and all lay in the fields and woods waiting for the KKK for three days. After three days, the owner of the property came and called to Daddy and said, "Henry, you can come out. Go get your family, no one will bother you." It was believed that he was a member of the KKK, and that my Daddy had some sort of connection with Mr. Magee's wife. Whenever Mr. Magee would fuss at my Daddy, she would always say, "Mentone, leave Henry alone."

It was good to be back home and with Daddy. After all, this was my senior year, and everyone was getting ready for graduation. I was named valedictorian and allowed to write my own speech. I don't rightly know where the words came from, but at the end, I received lots of hugs and congratulations. Attending my high school class reunion was great. It's not so bad to remember.

Queen in the center dressed in white

CHAPTER SIX

College Experiences

I graduated from high school with honors and was accepted to South Carolina State College (now University). I was happy, ready to leave home and especially the cotton fields. However, shortly after I received the acceptance letter, Daddy informed me there was no money for me to enroll at SCSC because my two older sisters were already in college. I cried for days.

Now, my sister Yvonne tells the story that there was a man called Cousin Buddie, and everyone thought he was homeless. Daddy would spend time with Cousin Buddie whenever he saw him, so he was something of a friend. On this day, Daddy was talking with him and told him his baby girl, me, wanted to go to college but he did not have the money. He asked Daddy how much he needed, and Daddy said $300. Cousin Buddie stood up and reached in his second pair of pants, pulled out his money belt, gave Daddy the money, and said, "Send that girl to college." Two months later, they found Cousin Buddie's body. Daddy believed that someone was watching when Cousin Buddie pulled out his money belt. No one ever knew what happened to him, but his money belt was gone. God may not come when you want him, but he is always on time, because Cousin Buddie really was God-sent.

So now I really was on my way to college. I recall that Daddy, Mom, my sister Yvonne, and my brothers Henry Jr. John Lewis, James Thomas, and Mentone took me to college. Mom fried chicken and made her favorite buttermilk biscuits, potato salad, and a jug of iced tea. On the way, Daddy saw a nice spot beside the road, and we stopped and had a picnic. There was no McDonald's, nor an interstate highway with roadside stops, but we still had lots of fun.

I knew I was really prepared for college, a smart girl like me. However, I did not realize there were smart kids from all over the state and some from out of state. In my classes, I realized how limited my experiences were. Regardless, I knew I would do my best, because that's what Henry and Lucille expected. I was competing against kids who later became doctors, lawyers, professors, teachers, politicians, etc. Yes the class of 61 produced outstanding individuals. In the picture I am on the second row, 2nd lady from left.

The picture below is a more recent picture from the class of '61 reunion.

Even after making it to college, there were still struggles. At the end of the first semester, I received a call from Daddy saying there was no money for me to continue in school. I cried for hours until I remembered what Mom always said: "Pick up your bootstraps and keep going." I did not understand what that meant until then. I went to my advisor and explained the situation to her. She sent me to the director of the dining hall, and I explained to her that I needed a job to stay in school. She looked at me and said, "I don't need another lazy student who don't want to work." I got up from the chair, with tears meeting under my chin. I looked at her and said loudly, "You don't have to give me a job, but I am going to get an education, and I am not a lazy student. I worked all my life on a farm as a sharecropper's daughter." I walked out of her office and slammed that door as hard as I could. Then I heard a voice saying, "Come back here, child, be in the dining hall at 12:00."

I had the job that would pay for room and board, and now I needed funds for tuition. I went to Ms. Poozer, the director's secretary, and asked her if she would type a note for me. The note went like this: "Dear Mr. Nance" – the director of business and finance – "my name is Queen Esther Berry, a sharecropper's daughter from Fountain Inn, SC. I am a rising second semester freshman and I don't have money for tuition. I just got a job paying for room and board, and if you would sign for me to register on a credit plan, I will pay you back."

Mr. Nance wanted to know if Daddy and Mom asked me to do this. I said, "No, they don't have the money." He asked, "Who will pay the money back?" Boldly, I said, "I will. With the help of God, I know I can." I think the word "God" got through to him; however, he said, "I can't do that." I followed him around the gym (where registration was taking place) for almost an hour. Every time he turned around, there I was, smiling in his face. Finally, he said, "Take this note to the business office and tell them to give you permission to register." As he walked away, I heard him say, "I know I am going to regret this." I said, "No you won't, because I will pay it back." Yes, God is always there.

After I had been working in the dining hall for two weeks, the director, Mrs. Sheffield, gave me a job at her house assisting with catering parties and sewing for her. I would go to her house after I finished working in the dining hall around 6:00 p.m., work until about 10:00, go back to the dorm, take a shower, and go to bed. Then I would get up around 4:00 a.m., go to the end of the hall where there was light, and get my homework out and study for the next day. Every month when I got my paycheck, I would take half to the business office to pay on my debt, then send Daddy and Mom a few dollars just to splurge – after all, they were still sharecroppers. I never forgot my roots. I studied hard and kept my grades up. When I got an F in History because I could not understand the professor's teaching style, I took the course over and made a B.

At the end of the first semester of my second year, for the Christmas holidays, I caught the Greyhound bus to go home. As I boarded the bus, I noticed a sign that said "NO NEGROES." I found a seat in the front row, just behind the sign. The front area filled up quickly, and then a white man got on the bus, looked at me, and said, "Nigger, get up and give me that seat." I wanted to slap him, but I remembered what Mom had said: "Keep your mouth shut and don't cause any trouble." I stood up for the 40 miles from Orangeburg to Columbia. When I changed buses in Columbia, I found a seat in back of the bus. However, when we arrived in Fountain Inn, I saw the sign at the water fountain that said "White Only" – another slap in the face.

Going home for Christmas was basically the same old thing, still a sharecropper's daughter. My brothers (Henry Jr. John Lewis, James, and Mentone) and I went to the cotton field to pick scrap cotton – cotton that was left in the field at the end of the season – to sell and get money for Christmas. Daddy told me to go to the big house and let them know we were outside. I went to the front door, and the owner's wife came to the door and looked at me as if I was from Mars. I spoke to her, but she said, "Go to the back door" and slammed the door in my face.

I informed my daddy of what happened, and he said, "Short Stuff, why did you do that?" I asked Daddy, "What did I do wrong?" He said, "You know you are supposed to go the back door. Don't let going to college mess you up. Your mom and I do this because we have to borrow money to send you to school."

For the first time, I realized the sacrifices Daddy and Mom made to provide for their children. They were humiliated, disrespected, dishonored, degraded, shamed, and sometimes treated as less than a human being. From that day, I prayed Daddy and Mom would soon leave the farm.

Yes, I was at SCSC when the student sit-in began. At that time, I was still working in the dining hall, and the director informed all the student workers that if we participated in the march, we would be fired. I really needed that job, so I asked her if there was anything else I could do. She said I could make sandwiches and gather blankets for the students in jail. Well, it wasn't what I wanted to do, but the students had to eat and keep warm. I was really hurt, because I really wanted to participate in the march. Sometimes we have to suffer the consequences.

The remainder of my college days were somewhat enjoyable. I joined the cheerleaders and traveled with the football team, cheering them to victory. I attended dances in Duke's Gymnasium and became Queen for the Agriculture Fellows, with my sister Yvonne as my attendant. Riding on that float in the homecoming parade was great, something I never dreamed of. I thought I looked pretty good as a QUEEN.

When it came time for graduation. I wasn't the smartest one in the class, but I graduated with honors. My family came, and as I walked across the stage, I could see the happy smiles on their faces. It was a great day. Shortly after I graduated, Daddy and Mom left the farm and McCarter Road. Daddy began working in a textile plant and Mom worked in a doctor's office. The boys were able to get odd jobs and finished high school.

Returning to my alma mater for a class reunion was bittersweet, – bitter because there were those who had passed away, and sweet for those who came. Trying to remember names was a task, so when we approached a class member, the first thing we did was to look at the name tag, making it seem as though we remembered. Those were the best of times.

CHAPTER SEVEN

Work Experiences

Queen B.

*M*y first job was in a small town in South Carolina, 18 miles from Orangeburg. To accept the job, I would need a car. Never forget your parents! Daddy took me to a car dealer he had done business with, talked with the man, co-signed, and I drove off in a red and white Ford. Daddy and Mom went with me to the small town to sign the contract and find a place to stay. The Agriculture teacher told us about a lady who was boarding two teachers and said that maybe she would take one more.

The following Monday, I went to visit the school and found that it was totally disappointing. Much of the equipment was not working: old stoves, old refrigerator, one working sewing machine. Everything was very old and unusable. I went to the principal's office to express my concerns and inquired about the budget for Home Economics, which had been my major in college. He informed me there was no budget. I remembered from my college days (never burn your bridges!) and my directed teaching class that the South Carolina State Department of Education allocated $2.50 per child enrolled. I kindly suggested this to him, but once again, he said there were no funds.

I drove to Orangeburg and discussed the situation with Mrs. Mattie E. Magee, the director of student teaching at SCSC. She said, "Child, he just did not understand what you were saying. Go and talk with him again." I did, and he continued to insist there was no money. I went back to Mrs. Magee, she told me to go to the superintendent and I did just that. He invited me in and said, "You do look like a little girl." I assumed that meant someone had been talking about me, but I did not follow up on that.

I remember my college professor said my looks would carry me a long way. I was allowed to see the home economics classroom in the white school. It was decked out. He agreed that there were monies available. He said, "Just fill these requisitions, get the principal to sign, and bring them back." When I carried the requisitions to the principal, he looked at them and began tearing them up in my face and said, "I told you there was no money. Now get out of my office and don't come back with this subject again."

I did not go back to Orangeburg this time; I felt this was something I had to handle on my own. I rewrote the requisitions and carried them to the superintendent, and he signed them and told me to send them to the vendors. I really did not like the way he looked at me, so I stayed my distance. By that point, it was time for Christmas holidays, so I went home. I spoke with one of my older sisters, Dorothy, and told her I was not going back. She insisted that you just don't walk off your first job. So I went back, and two weeks after I returned, trucks started rolling in with all the equipment and supplies I had ordered. Afterward, though, the principal sent me a letter informing me that my services were no longer needed after May 31, 1962. There I was – fired from my first job. Daddy and Mom told me that my mouth and actions would get me in trouble one day. This was one time I was glad my mouth and actions got me in trouble, because those kids needed that change. Thanks be to God.

After losing the job in the town, I heard about a job in Sparta, Georgia. I called and was asked to come for an interview, which I did, still relying on Daddy and Mom to go with me. The principal said he was impressed with my future plan for Home Economics, but he needed a recommendation from my former employer. I reminded him I was fired, but he said it didn't matter, it could either be a good or not-so-good recommendation. He further stated that it would be left to him to make the final decision. After the interview, the principal from Sparta called me and said that my former principal would not give me a recommendation and he had to hire someone else.

My sister said she would get me a job where she worked, so I talked with my boyfriend, Nicholas Brailey, who later became my husband, and informed him that I was going to California. The day before I would have gotten my flight ticket, my boyfriend called and said there was a Home Economics position available in Cross, South Carolina. I made contact with the principal, Rev. S.B. Marshall, and he scheduled an interview, He also said the school district required a letter of reference from my previous employer, and I explained to him that my former employer would not give me a reference. He asked if I knew of anyone else who might give me one. When I mentioned Mrs. Mattie E, Magee, he said he would take a letter of recommendation from her any day.

I contacted Mrs. Magee and explained the situation. She said, "On your way to Cross, stop by my office, I will have the letter ready," and she had a three-page letter. A lesson for those who read this book: don't burn your bridges. I got the job and worked there for three successful years. Two years into that job, I married the guy who was responsible for me getting the job, and one year later, I moved to Orangeburg. My husband did not like me driving 50 miles each way every day, so I resigned in May 1967.

Picture Left to Right. Mr. & Mrs. Nicholas Brailey, Queen, Rev. Curry in background, Nick his brother Isaac and Mr. & Mrs. Henry Berry

One year after coming to Orangeburg, I was faced with the Orangeburg massacre on February 8, 1968. I was nines month pregnant and living with a curfew. My husband and I began to plot a route for how to get to the hospital in case the baby came. However, she waited until February 24 to make her entrance. We were saddened by the massacre but overjoyed by our baby girl, Necole Michele Brailey.

Our one-bedroom apartment became a little crowded, so I began looking for another job to assist my husband in saving money to buy a house. My neighbor, Mary Moorer, secretary to the president of South Carolina State College (now University), informed me of a position on the campus. I was excited and overjoyed that I was returning to my alma mater, only to find out the position was for a nutritionist at the preschool. Three hours from my master's degree and I ended up a cook. Going back to my roots and remembering what my mom once said, "Always do the best in whatever you end up doing," I accepted the position and prepared the best meals the kids would ever get – after all, my BS degree was in Home Economics. It was during this time I realized the gift God had blessed me with: taking care of children, training teachers and parents in early childhood concepts.

However, staying in that position was one of the hardest jobs I ever had. I was there for six years. It was as if I were stuck in that red clay from Greenville County, but I knew God had not brought me that far to leave me. God had a bigger plan for me. He said, "Wait and it shall be given," and wait I did. After the six years passed, one of my former professors, Dr. Annabelle Sherman Boykin, returned to the college. She wanted to know why they graduated me with a BS degree only to give me that position.

Dr. Boykin, I was told, assisted in writing the National Head Start Grant. That summer, she recommended me for the position of Education Director of the Summer Head Start (H/S) Program in Summerton, South Carolina. Yes! My husband and I purchased property and began building our home. At the end of that summer, Dr. Boykin hosted a statewide Head Start Directors conference on the campus of South Carolina State College, and she requested that I assist her. Around that same time, it was announced that the H/S state training office had been relocated from the University of South Carolina to South Carolina State College, and the position of director needed to be filled. I was named director. *OUT OF THE RED MUD!* For the first time, I felt like I was out of my league. But being a sharecropper's daughter, and with everything God had carried me through to get to this point, I would not give up.

I became concerned about not having administrative training, so I discussed it with Dr. Boykin. She informed me that she would give me an administrative course if I would just come to her office each day at four o'clock. The course was real life experiences, beginning at the governor's office. She named individuals I could go to when I needed help. She also talked about my looks and said being pretty was a plus – "Use it, but never forget you have a beautiful family."

I consider myself a brave woman. However, when I was presented with a ticket to fly to Atlanta, Georgia, it was scary. I had never flown before, but I was confident I could do it. When I arrived at the meeting, I could hear Training Officers from other states making statements like, "Why do we come to these meetings? We don't get anything from them and it's just a waste of time."

There was an older white gentleman in the group. He came over to me – I guess I was looking like a scared rabbit – and asked if I had plans for lunch. I didn't know whether or not to accept, but I did – God had always led me in the right direction. At lunch, he talked about some of the work they were doing in North Carolina, and when we finished, he got up and said, "I have a philosophy I would like to share with you, and that is, wherever I go or whatever meetings I attend, I go with the idea that I will get something from it," and he walked away. I have kept his philosophy throughout my life.

At the meeting, I was given several notebooks with information from the H/S regional office to go back and inform SC head directors of their content. After staying up several nights reading and preparing myself for the meeting with the directors, I just knew I was ready. But fifteen minutes into the meeting, they began looking at me as if I was from Mars . I immediately called for a coffee break. Not knowing what I was going to do, I went to the restroom, threw my hands in the air, and said, "God, why did you bring me this far to leave me?" He had not left me but was carrying me. When I walked out of the bathroom, there stood one of the Head Start directors. He looked at me and said, "Do you know what you are doing?" I said, "I thought I did." He informed me that they received that information several weeks ago.

I said, "What do you suggest I do?" He said, "When we go back inside, pick up from where you left off. I will raise my hand, you recognize me, and the three other directors will take it from there." Now, you tell me if that wasn't the work of God. I made it to the end of the meeting and together we developed a state training plan.

A few weeks later, I returned to Atlanta for another briefing. I was informed by my Atlanta supervisor, Mr. Edward Vaughn, that Dr. Boykin, the lady responsible for hiring me, was leaving South Carolina State College. When I returned and asked her if it was true that she was leaving, her answer was yes. My response was, "What am I supposed to do?" She said, "I gave you your wings, you can fly or you can fall. Now get out of my office." I was forced to fly. Shortly after her departure, at a South Carolina State Head Start conference, I was told by the Head Start Regional Director that a letter had been prepared by state officials to apply for a block grant. The director said that this grant would put Head Start under the State Department of Education, and that I must do something.

As this was my first time being exposed to politics, I talked with a few Head Start Directors, and they suggested I talk with State Representative Hubert Fielding, who was in attendance. I did, and he was sure there was no such letter. I wondered why a lady would risk her job to tell me that, but he continued to insist that there was no letter. During this discussion with Rep. Fielding, I received a phone call from my husband, telling me that my daughter was sick with the chickenpox and running a high fever and I must come home. I left immediately to go and take care of my daughter. I was up with her all night, and at about four o'clock that morning, Rep. Fielding called and said they had found the letter, and that I needed to return. I talked with my husband and we agreed that if his mother, who lived next door, would come over and help with the baby, I would go back to the conference.

When I arrived at the conference, the next morning Rep. Fielding was waiting for me. Little old me, the sharecropper's daughter getting into politics. He wanted to know what I was going to do. I called together a group of Head Start employees, Rep. Fielding, and the Director of Head Start Supplementary Training, Dr. Amelia Adams, and we developed a resolution. The resolution addressed the goals and objectives of Head Start versus those of the State Department of Education. Head Start leaned heavily on a comprehensive services approach that included Parent Involvement, Social Services, Mental Health, Nutrition, Medical and Dental and Special Needs Services addressing the total needs of children and their families.

We were successful, and Head Start was still in its rightful place with the Community Action Agencies (CAP). The next year, my second daughter was born. I called her my Head Start baby. I was confronted with one more major training task with Head Start, developing a plan for implementing Management By Objectives (MBO) in all Head Start programs.

The Head Start Grant finally came to an end, and the funds were decentralized to local programs. Instead of returning to the preschool as the cook, I returned as Director. After the birth of my second child, I saw the need for more quality child care. That summer, I began an all-day six-week program in my garage for children in first through sixth grades. Right away I enrolled fifteen children, all that I could accommodate. At the conclusion of the program, parents were urging me to open a child care and an afternoon program.

In 1978, still employed at SCSC, I decided to try my hand at entrepreneurship, so I rented a house from a good friend, Dr. Jessie Kinard, across the street from SCSC. It took what my mom called "elbow grease" to prepare the house for occupancy. At the time, my husband was totally against it, but with my persuasive attitude, it did not take long to convince him.

The center, Kid's World Learning Center, was licensed for 40 children, and after a few weeks, it was filled to capacity. I didn't really make money, and when I did, I put it right back into the program. The program provided jobs for Claflin and SCSC students, as well as for my two daughters for a short while until they found other jobs that would provide better benefits. The center also provided parent training and served as a laboratory for students majoring in Child Development and Early Childhood at the two colleges.

I recall getting in debt with the IRS for not paying taxes on time. Well, I thought paying my staff came first. Wrong decision. The IRS paid me a visit and posted my building and stated that the post must remain on the door. He was really mean and cruel.

The next morning, the sign had been taken down. I asked Mrs. Shuler (the staff member who would take care of business and always had my back), "What happened to the sign?" With a straight face, she replied, "I don't know." So I asked Mrs. Zimmerman and Mrs. Quatterbaum, who also had my back: "What happened to the sign?" Finally they said, "Mrs. Brailey, as hard as you work, they don't have the right to do this." My reply was, "Yes they do, so I must pay it, which means you all will have to wait two weeks without pay for me to do this." Of course, you know they did.

Mrs. Shuler and Right Mrs. Zimmerman, Mrs. Quattlebaum not pictured

After 23 years, Kid's World closed its doors. It became too hard to maintain good staff and pay what they deserved and to give the children the type of service I was used to providing.

I remained in a relationship with Ed Vaughn – remember, my supervisor when I was director of the H/S state training office. He informed me of an available grant that SCSC might be interested in applying for. I discussed it with my supervisors, and we applied for and received the grant. The grant was designed to provide training for Head Start education staff in implementing the HighScope Curriculum. The training lasted one year, which was also the year of my mother's death. Thirteen H/S Education Coordinators, including myself, were endorsed as HighScope Trainers. Together we planned a statewide conference, inviting H/S staff, public school teachers, and staff from the State

Department of Education, national and regional Head Start, the State Office of Child Development, and local day care centers.

Planning the meeting, I suggested the idea of inviting the owner of the curriculum, Dr. David Weikart. Most did not believe he would come, being an international consultant. But God said to present your plan, seek counsel, and wait for the answer. It took a few days before I was able to get him on the phone. I explained to him that the State of South Carolina Head Start had completed training in the HighScope Curriculum and was planning a statewide conference, and that we wanted him to give the keynote address.

He said, "Lady, do you know what my fee is?" I said, "No. However, we will be using your curriculum and most of your materials needed to implement it. It would be a real boost to our state to have you come. I am sure you know South Carolina is 47th on the educational ladder, and we know that improvement begins at the preschool level." He asked, "How much can you afford?" I said we can give you per diem and travel. He laughed and said, "I don't know why I am entertaining this conversation." Well, I told him I didn't think it was funny, because South Carolina was 47th in the nation, and his research showed that a child involved in a high-quality early childhood program almost always finishes high school and continues through college. He agreed to come. Over 500 participants came. The HighScope curriculum became the standard for Head Start, some kindergarten programs, and day care for many years. I think this curriculum went over big because it allowed children to actively participate in their own learning.

Based on my experiences, I not only continued as Director of the preschool but became Instructor of Child Development at SCSC and taught Child Development classes until my retirement.

CHAPTER EIGHT

Retirement

I retired at age 51, ready to begin a new phase of my life, enjoy my commitment to my Sorority "AKA," and serve as a role model for my daughters.

Daughter Crystal and Queen

However, I was asked to return to the university and teach Early Childhood classes. Me, the sharecropper's daughter, in demand. I had truly established my credibility. I recall that in one of my classes, a Freshman Seminar class, there was a young lady who refused to sit up in her chair.

She was asked several times to sit up, but as soon as I walked away, she would resume the same position. I finally put her out of my class. One of the professors, whose office was next to mine, told me that if I was not careful, one of those students was going to attack me. My reply was, "If we don't correct them here, it will never happen. I will take my chance."

The next morning, the young lady and her mother were standing outside my office door. Yes, big bad me was a little frightened! Her mother said, "I want to know why you put my child out of your class." I looked at the student and said, "You explain it to your mother, and this time, tell the truth." Her mother looked at her and said, "You better tell the truth." My classroom was across from my office, so I suggested we move to the classroom. I said to the student, "Show your mother how you sit in class." I finally got her to show her mother. Her mother slapped her in the face and said, "You had me come from Charleston on a lie. You make things right with Mrs. Brailey." The next morning, the student came to class and apologized. I informed her that I was there to teach not only the course work but the manners that go along with becoming an excellent Early Childhood teacher. She became one of my best students. We must give the students the best that we have, even if there is a threat to our being.

Another incident was when one of my 260lbs football players came to class late. I was standing in the doorway, and he appeared in an undershirt and tried to squeeze past me. I informed him he could not come to my class in that shirt. I said, "You will have respect for the ladies in this class. You can go back to the dorm and get another shirt, or you can drop from this class." He went back, came back with a beautiful shirt on, and got a standing ovation from his classmates. He looked at me and said, "You remind me of my mother." He said, "I am sorry." Sometimes older students need a little push in the right direction.

41

Furthering my commitment to improving programs for young children and their families, I agreed to direct the Berkeley/Dorchester/Charleston County Head Start in South Carolina. The program was in jeopardy of losing its funding and required that an improvement plan be developed. I engaged Edward Vaughn, and together we put the program in good standing.

In 2006 I was named to the board of directors of First Steps, a state-funded program for four-year-old children, and to the South Carolina steering committee for child abuse. When my church needed me, I stepped in and served on the board for the child care center and as a special consultant for the center. In addition, we began a summer program for young children and applied for USDA funding for free food for those children, as well as children in the surrounding areas.

The great surprise was when my daughter came up with the idea to give me a 75th birthday celebration. It was the first time in my life I was surprised.

Queen and daughter Crystal

Granddaughters Jamauri, Aubrai, Queen and grandson James

State Representative Jerry Govan, presenting a State Proclamation

Sisters and brothers - from left – Yvonne, Queen,
Dorothy and James Thomas (Jim)

Dancing with nephew Harold Dial

Crystal, Serenity, Aubrai, and Jamauri

Queen 5th from left

Crystal invited over 200 people, and they all came and signed the photo frame. I never thought I had touched so many lives. One of the happiest evenings of my life.

CHAPTER NINE

Church Affiliations

The church has always been an anchor in my life. I was born into the Baptist church, where I was taught the Bible through the Sunday school and church services. When I was in college, Mt. Zion Church in Fountain Inn, SC, would send me ten or twenty dollars a month. What a blessing that was to be remembered in such a positive manner. I maintained my relationship with the Baptist church until I married Nicholas Brailey.

My husband was Methodist and was very active in the church. After much thought and learning the history of Trinity United Methodist Church in Orangeburg, SC, I moved my membership from the Baptist church to the Methodist church.

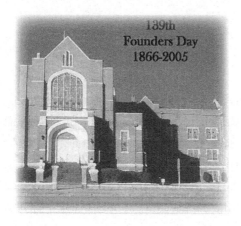

139th
Founders Day
1866-2005

According to the church's website, Trinity has served as a spiritual haven for students from South Carolina State University, Claflin University, and the Orangeburg community. The church has been a focal point for community service programs; its members have been in the vanguard of civic improvement projects. Further, the church was named to the National Register of Historic Places in January 1995. I felt it an honor to become a part of such a prestigious group of Christian believers. Trinity has allowed me to work and express my skills in many Christian ways.

I became a Sunday school teacher. One Sunday in the spring, we lifted the window to allow a cool breeze to come in. It just so happened that we were discussing how God is everywhere. Just at that moment, a cool breeze came through the window. One of the very young children jumped in my lap and said, "Is that God?" That breeze proved my point.

48

I served as Director of Trinity United Methodist Church Child Care Learning Center for one year, bringing it into compliance with USDA. In addition, I met a man from the South Carolina Office of Child Development, Mr. Robert Coffey with whom I discussed the possibility of getting a bus for the center to allow children to go on field trips. He suggested I write a grant for $5,000 as a down payment. Then, the church and the child care center made the balance of the payments.

Continuing my involvement with child care, I ran a summer enrichment program for children ages six through twelve with three other women from the church: Barbara Bowman Nesmith, PhD, Vera Graham, and Evelyn Hubbard. Activities included swimming, tennis, reading, math, health, and field trips – making sure we used the bus!

Children's Sabbath was my next adventure. It is a national interfaith program sponsored by the National Children's Defense Fund. This effort was coordinated through the United Methodist Women organization of Trinity United Methodist Church. The Program included a march from downtown Orangeburg to Trinity's parking lot. The focus was to bring the attention of the community to the injustices happening to our children and to leave no child behind. The march and program drew over 100 participants. They came from different churches, Boy Scouts, the child care center, South Carolina State and Claflin Universities, middle and high school, and fraternities and sororities. Speakers came from different disciplines: Law Enforcement, Mental Health, Department of Social Services, Child Protective Services, Department of Juvenile Justice, and clergy.

Rev. McCutcheon lead group participants on a March from down town
Orangeburg to Trinity United Methodist Church.
This was in celebration of children Sabbath

January 29, 2017, was the first meeting of Mothers and Daughters In Christ. This program was an outgrowth of a women's Bible study group of which I am a member. Vera Graham chairs the group, and the other members include Ophelia Montgomery, Myra Thomas, Priscilla Jarvis, Annetta Clowney, Mildred Rose, Marsha Rose Randolph, Grace Salter, Betty Wilson, and Gloria Dean. For months, we studied the women of the Bible, ate food, and went home. One day, during the regular Bible study, we realized we were not doing all that God wanted us to do. He wanted us to do more than just reading, studying, and eating. So we decided to think about it until the next meeting. The day before the next meeting, God gave me a vision: to work with mothers and their daughters. I presented it to the group, and it became "Mothers and Daughters in Christ." The first meeting, we sat and waited for someone to show, and finally one mother and her daughter came, What a HALLELUJAH good time it was. The group has now grown from one mother and daughter to seven.

Our stated purpose is derived from Titus 2:3-5 in the Bible: *"Likewise, teach the older women to be reverent in the way they live, not to be slanderers or addicted to much wine, but to teach what is good. Then they can urge the younger women to love their husbands and children, to be self-controlled and pure, to be busy at home, to be kind, and to be subject to their husbands, so that no one will malign the word of God."* Our goal is to provide spiritual guidance to young girls in sixth through ninth grades and their mothers. It addresses problems facing mothers and daughters on a daily basis: teenage pregnancy, education, low wages for women, lack of young women interested in STEM careers. Specific objectives include but are not limited to the following:

1. Spiritual growth and prayer
2. Enhancing self-esteem
3. Developing leadership skills
4. Establishing long-range plans
5. Building a strong relationship between mothers and daughters
6. Participating in community outreach projects

Our most exciting outreach project was collecting funds to donate to Operation Smile. This organization, according to their literature, is an international medical charity that has provided hundreds of thousands of free surgeries for children and young adults who are born with cleft lip, cleft palate or other facial deformities. It is one of the oldest and largest volunteer-based organizations dedicated to improving the health and lives of children worldwide through access to surgical care. The children and parents of Trinity United Methodist Church Child Care Center also helped out by putting together care packages to give to children in the hospital. This included coloring books, crayons, toothbrushes, toothpaste, books, etc. The total monetary gift from Mothers and Daughters in Christ was $400.00, enough for two operations.

Mother and Daughters in Christ Workshop

EPILOGUE

Writing this book has been one of the most satisfying, memorable, rewarding, and exciting adventures of my life. After hearing the way I used my life experiences in making a presentation to early childhood educators, my daughters, Necole and Crystal, felt it should be shared not only with the family, but with those who are experiencing difficulty in school, college, and early employment.

In sharing my experiences with the public, I hope that those who read this book come to the conclusion that nothing in life is impossible. I believe my daughters realized for the first time that the life of a sharecropper's daughter was sometimes very hard; however, they realized that out of the hard times came success. In addition, they felt it would give me something to do as I recover from taking Rituxan and chemo. Yes, I have cancer! However, cancer doesn't have me. After all, God has blessed me beyond distance. How many 81-year-olds can say God has allowed them to live and see four generations?

TO GOD BE THE GLORY

Queen's
FAMILY TREE

Henry & Lucille Berry's
FAMILY TREE

Family Tree

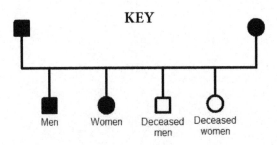

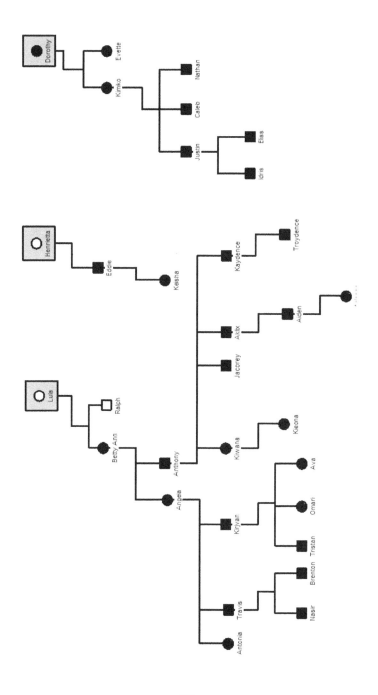

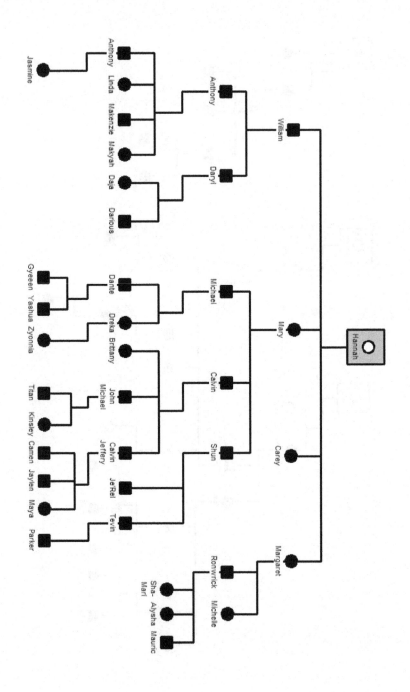

60

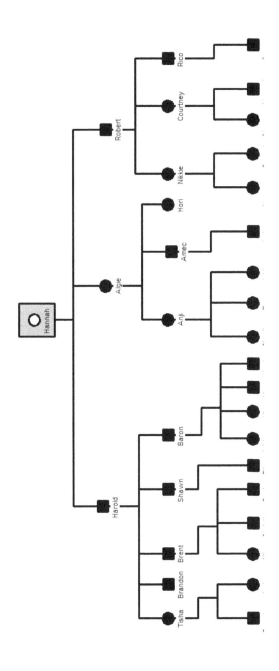

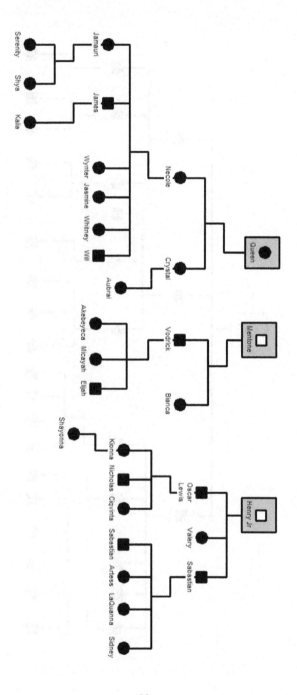

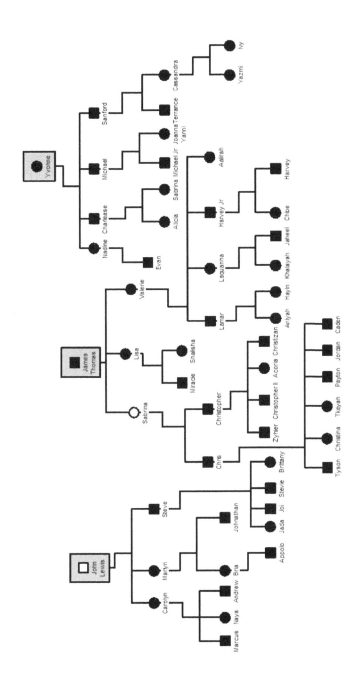

What a joy
it has been
to walk down
memory lane.

Queen

.

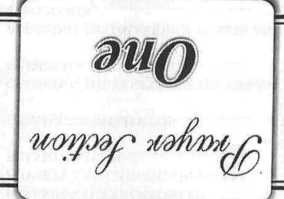

Prayer Section

One

PRAYER OF THANKSGIVING

INTRODUCTION:

Ps. 136:1 *"O give thanks unto the Lord, for he is good, for his mercies endureth forever."*
It is good to give thanks unto the Lord at all times. Many times as Christians, we often rush through giving of thanks in the place of prayer, but it is important to give him praise and not just bring our requests only when we pray. Therefore, take time to appreciate God as you take this prayers from a heart overflowing with deep gratitude.

CONFESSION: PSALM 136

Praise Worship

Prayer Points

1. Father, I praise Your Holy name for bearing my burdens on daily basis.
2. O God, I thank You for You are the Refiner.
3. O God, I thank You for the greatness of Your works.
4. O God, I thank You for You are the Sun of Righteousness.
5. O God, I thank You for You are a great God and King over all gods.

6. My Father, I thank You for being my Physician.
7. Great Father of Glory, I thank You because on Your hands are the depths of the earth, and the mountain peaks belong to You.
8. My Father, I thank You for You are my Messiah.
9. O God, I thank You for the marvelous things You have done.
10. Father, thank You for being my Prophet.
11. O God, I thank You for redeeming my life from the pit and crowning me with compassion and love.
12. O Lord, I thank You for being the Strength of my soul.
13. O God, I thank You for satisfying my desires with good things so that my strength is renewed like the eagle's.
14. O God, I thank You for being my Cornerstone.
15. Father, I thank You for making the cloud Your chariots and for riding on the wings of the wind.
16. Father, You are praised for being the Great High Priest.
17. Father, glory be to Your Holy name for making the winds Your messengers and Your ministers flames of fire.
18. My Father, I thank You for being the Bishop of my Soul.
19. O God, I thank You for You set the earth on its foundation and it can never be moved.
20. O God, I thank You for You are the God of all Grace.
21. O God, I thank You for great are Your works, pondered on by all who delight in them.

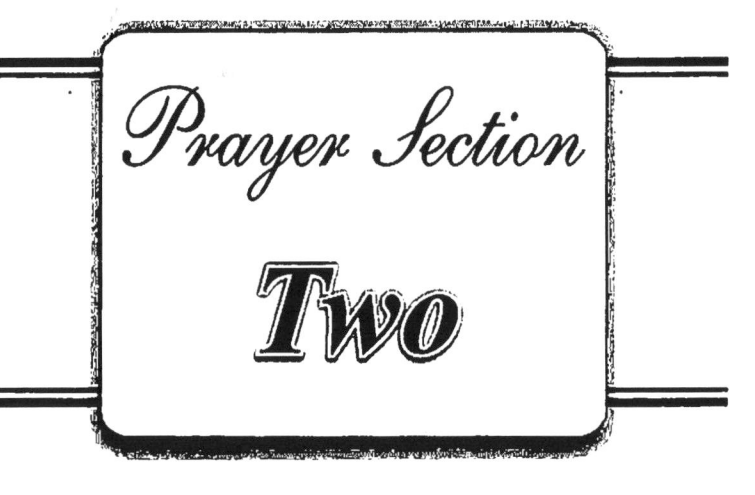

Prayer Section

Two

PRAYER OF PURGING

INTRODUCTION

The body of a man can be likened to a container which can be filled with things, both good or bad. Like the Gadarene demoniac has shown, the body has enormous capacity as demonstrated by the fact that he alone had about 6000 demons. Imagine if such a life is totally yielded to the Holy Spirit! These prayers are for cleansing from every pollution emanating from food, drink, eating in the dream, sex, wrong books, films and the like; and they will ensure that your life's vessel is clean from all these evil so that you can receive the blessing which God has intended for you without any hindrance.

CONFESSION: Matt. 15:13 *"But he answered and said, Every tree which my heavenly Father has not planted, shall be rooted up."*

Praise Worship

Prayer Points

1. Thank God for being the God that answers prayers.
2. Confess every known sin in your life and ask for the mercy of God.
3. Cover yourself with the blood of Jesus.
4. Every word, vision and dream that did not originate from the Holy Spirit, I render you null and void, in the name of Jesus.

5. Every tree that God the Father has not planted in my life, be uprooted by fire, in the name of Jesus.
6. Every power of darkness assigned against my life, die, in the name of Jesus.
7. I use the blood of Jesus to insulate my spirit and soul from all demonic influences, in the name of Jesus.
8. Every power of darkness using my dreams to manipulate my life, die, in the name of Jesus.
9. Let the angels of God gather heavenly resources to fight all my adversaries, in the name of Jesus.
10. Every evil spirit that has attacked me in the dream, die, in the name of Jesus.
11. Every evil prophecy and negative pronouncement over my life, be cancelled by the power in the blood of Jesus, in the name of Jesus.
12. I renounce every familiar spirit, and I reject their covenants, in the name of Jesus.
13. Every spirit of death and grave, lose your hold upon my life, in the name of Jesus.
14. Every curse of untimely death upon my life, break, by the blood of Jesus, in the name of Jesus.
15. Every agent of the spirit of death assigned against my life, be arrested, in the name of Jesus.
16. Every harassment of the spirit of death in my dreams, die, in the name of Jesus.
17. Every arrow of death and destruction, go back to your senders, in the name of Jesus.

18. I shall not die, I shall live long, the number of my days shall be fulfilled to declare the works of God, in the name of Jesus.
19. Every coffin prepared for my life, catch your owner, in the name of Jesus.
20. Every satanic funeral procession organized against me, scatter, in the name of Jesus.
21. Every satanic poison in my body, melt away by the blood of Jesus.
22. Every arrow of pain and sickness, go back to your sender, in the name of Jesus.
23. Every arrow of weakness and disease, go back to your sender, in the name of Jesus.
24. Every arrow of insanity and suffering, go back to your sender, in the name of Jesus.
25. My body, eject every satanic poison, in the name of Jesus.
26. Every disease planted into my body through dreams, come out and die, in the name of Jesus.
27. Every spiritual poison in my body, I eject you by the blood of Jesus, in the name of Jesus.
28. Every effort of the enemy to weaken my prayer altar, be frustrated, in the name of Jesus.
29. Every unclean spirit assigned to be polluting my body in the dreams, die, in the name of Jesus.
30. Every spirit spouse assigned to be molesting me in the dreams, die, in the name of Jesus.

31. Let the thunder and lightning of God blind every spirit spouse in the name of Jesus.
32. Every spirit of immorality, wickedness and witchcraft manifesting in form of dogs and serpents in my dreams, die, in the name of Jesus.
33. I barricade my life and home with the fire of God against the operations of spirit spouses, in Jesus' name.
34. Every remains from spirit spouse in my body, be flushed out by the blood of Jesus.
35. Every dream of backwardness, die, in the name of Jesus.
36. Every power using my dreams to hold back my progress in life, die, in the name of Jesus.
37. Every garment of backwardness, I reject you, catch fire, in the name of Jesus.
38. I bind and cast out every spirit of limitation, in the name of Jesus.
39. Every satanic cloth of non-achievement, you are not my portion, I reject you, catch fire, in Jesus' name.
40. Every gathering where my downfall is being discussed, arrows of fire, scatter them, in the name of Jesus.
41. Every satanic verdict of demotion for my life, catch fire in the name of Jesus.
42. All the blessings the Lord has given unto me shall remain with me for life, in the name of Jesus.
43. In every area of life, I shall not be demoted, in the name of Jesus.

44. This year, shame shall not know my life and my habitation, in the name of Jesus.
45. Every known and unknown covenant of water spirits for my life, be cancelled by the blood of Jesus.
46. Every water where I have swam in the dream, dry up by fire, in the name of Jesus.
47. Every spirit that has been oppressing me in the dream, die, in the name of Jesus.
48. Every dream of hopelessness, die, in the name of Jesus.
49. Every senseless and meaningless dream, die, in the name of Jesus.
50. Every negative dream shall not come to pass in my life, in the name of Jesus.
51. Every spiritual cannibal, vomit everything you have eaten from my life in the name of Jesus.
52. Every spirit behind evil dreams in my life, die, in the name of Jesus.
53. Let the finger of God unseat my household strongman, in the name of Jesus.
54. I bind the strongman in my life, and I clear my goods from your possession, in the name of Jesus.
55. You strongman of mind destruction, be bound, in Jesus' name.
56. You strongman of financial destruction, be bound, in Jesus' name.

57. Every strongman of bad luck attached to my life, fall down and die, in Jesus' name

58. Every strongman assigned to weaken my faith, catch fire, in the name of Jesus

59. I bind every strongman delegated to hinder my progress, in the name of Jesus.

60. I bind the strongman behind my spiritual blindness and deafness and paralyze his operations in my life, in the name of Jesus.

61. Every ancestral covenant affecting my life, break and lose your hold, in the name of Jesus.

62. Every inherited family covenants affecting my life, break and lose your hold, in the name of Jesus.

63. Every inherited covenant affecting my life, break and release me, in the name of Jesus.

64. Any evil covenant prospering in my family, be broken by the blood of Jesus.

65. Every soul tie and covenant between me and ancestral spirit, break and release me, in the name of Jesus.

66. Every soul tie and covenant with any dead relations, break now and release me, in the name of Jesus.

67. Every soul tie and covenant with family gods, shrines and spirit break now and release me, in Jesus' name.

68. Every soul tie and covenant between me and my parents, break and release me, in the name of Jesus.

69. Every soul tie between me and my grandparents, break and release me, in the name of Jesus.

70. Every soul tie covenant between me and former boyfriends or girlfriends, break and lose your hold, in the name of Jesus.
71. Every soul tie covenant between me and any spirit husband or wife, break and lose your hold, in Jesus' name.
72. Every soul tie covenant between me and any demonic ministers, break and lose your hold, in Jesus' name.
73. Every soul tie covenant between me and my former house, office and/or, school, break and lose your hold, in the name of Jesus.
74. Every soul tie covenant between me and water spirit, break and lose your hold, in the name of Jesus.
75. Every soul tie covenant between me and serpentine spirit, break and lose your hold, in the name of Jesus.
76. Any covenant empowering my household enemy, break and lose your hold, in the name of Jesus.
77. Every soul tie covenant between me and any occultic relation break and lose your hold, in Jesus' name.
78. Every soul tie covenant between me and any dead relation, break and lose your hold, in the name of Jesus.
79. Any evil covenant strengthening the foundation of any bondage, be broken, in the name of Jesus.
80. Every soul tie covenant between me and familiar spirit, break and lose your hold, in the name of Jesus.
81. Every soul tie covenant between me and spiritual night caterers, break and lose your hold, in Jesus' name.

82. Every soul tie covenant between me and any territorial spirit, break and lose your hold, in Jesus' name.
83. Every soul tie covenant between me and any demonic church I have ever attended, break and lose your hold, in the name of Jesus.
84. Every soul tie covenant between me and any herbalist, break and lose your hold, in the name of Jesus.
85. Every soul tie covenant between me and the marine kingdom, break and lose your hold, in the name of Jesus.
86. Every soul tie covenant between me and witchcraft spirits, break and lose your hold, in the name of Jesus.
87. Every soul tie covenant between me and the spirit of barrenness, break and lose your hold, in Jesus' name
88. Every soul tie covenant between me and the spirit of poverty, break and lose your hold, in the name of Jesus.
89. Every soul tie covenant between me and the spirit of infirmity and sickness, break and lose your hold, in the name of Jesus.
90. Every soul tie covenant between me and the spirit of insanity, break and lose your hold, in Jesus' name.
91. Every soul tie covenant between me and the spirit of backwardness and demotion, break and lose your hold, in the name of Jesus.
92. Every soul tie covenant between me and the spirit of failure, break and lose your hold, in Jesus' name.
93. Blood of Jesus, purify my spirit, soul and body in the name of Jesus.

94. Every evil spiritual deposit in my body, be ejected in the name of Jesus.
95. Every material of the enemy hiding in any part of my body, be flushed out by the blood of Jesus.
96. Begin to thank the Lord for answering your prayers.

Prayer Section

Three

DELIVERANCE OF THE SPIRIT, SOUL, AND BODY

INTRODUCTION

Genesis 2:7, Ecclesiastes 12:7. The soul, spirit and body can be defiled in many ways.

THE SPIRIT- Pollution comes into the spirit man through certain experiences such as eating in the dream, swimming or moving inside water, going to the toilet or walking and sitting in dung or dirty places. Having sexual intercourse in the dream is another common and easy way the enemy uses to contaminate both the spirit, soul and the body.

THE SOUL- The soul could become impure by filthy thoughts, lusts, hatred, bitterness etc.in the heart.

THE BODY- Impurity comes into the body through the application of body members to sin, e.g watching corrupt films and programmes that defile the body and soul. Eating and drinking in forbidden places such as idol temples, shrines, clubs, night parties, reading occultic books, sexual books, pornography and living in polluted houses and environment etc.

CONFESSION

Luke 13:12: *And when Jesus saw her, he called her to him, and said unto her, Woman, thou art loosed from thine infirmity.*
Acts 10:38: *How God anointed Jesus of Nazareth with the Holy Ghost and with power: who went about doing good, and healing all*

Praise Worship

Prayer Points

1. Thank the Lord, because He is the bondage breaker and the Great Physician.
2. Oh God arise and inject the blood of Jesus into my blood stream, in the name of Jesus.
3. Holy Ghost fire, purge every defilement away from my life, in the name of Jesus.
4. Anything planted in my body to oppress me, come out now, in the name of Jesus.
5. Any curse operating upon any organ of my body, break, in the name of Jesus.
6. I decree every authority assigned to torment me to expire, in the name of Jesus.
7. Every programme of affliction for my body and destiny, expire, in the name of Jesus.
8. Anything I have eaten or swallowed that is chaining me inside, I vomit them by fire, in the name of Jesus.
9. Blood of Jesus, Holy Ghost fire, sanitize my body, soul and spirit, in the name of Jesus.
10. Every wicked handwriting, operating in my bodily organs, be wiped off by the blood of Jesus.
11. My body, hear the word of the Lord, reject every arrow of darkness, in the name of Jesus.

12. Any tree that the Father has not planted inside my body, be uprooted by fire, in the name of Jesus.
13. Voice of the Almighty, speak wholeness into every department of my life, in the name of Jesus.
14. Divine power of creativity and repair, operate in my life now, in the name of Jesus.
15. My Father, cause every instrument of affliction in my body to expire, in the name of Jesus.
16. Any evil hand laid upon any organ of my body, wither, in the name of Jesus.
17. I reject totally, any bewitchment of any organ of my body, in the name of Jesus.
18. My Father, carry out a divine surgery that will move my life forward upon me, in the name of Jesus.
19. Any power cooking my spirit man in a caldron, fall down and die, in the name of Jesus.
20. Every internal yoke assigned against me, break, in the name of Jesus.
21. Satanic summon of my spirit man in a crystal ball or a dark mirror, backfire, in the name of Jesus.
22. Every evil hand fashioned to manipulate my life, catch fire, in the name of Jesus.
23. Every evil load in any part of my body, go back to your senders, in the name of Jesus.
24. Where is the Lord God of Elijah? Arise and kill every poison in my body, in the name of Jesus.

25

25. Every hidden infirmity and silent sickness, die, in the name of Jesus.
26. Every rage of the enemy assigned to send me backward, break, in the name of Jesus.
27. Every dark incantation, uttered against my wholeness, backfire, in the name of Jesus.
28. You eaters of flesh and drinkers of blood assigned against me, eat your flesh and drink your blood, in the name of Jesus.
29. Rain of affliction assigned to trouble my life, carry your warfare back to the enemy, in the name of Jesus.
30. Every evil mountain confronting my body, I cast you into the sea, in the name of Jesus.
31. Any power circulating my name for evil, carry your load, in the name of Jesus.
32. Every internal chain, suffocating my life, break, in the name of Jesus.
33. By the power that breaks the gates of brass and cuts the bars of iron asunder, let all my spiritual chains break, in the name of Jesus.
34. Any power organized to disorganize me; I bury you alive, in the name of Jesus.
35. Thank the Lord for answering your prayers.
36. Thank God for His mighty power to save to the uttermost and for the power to deliver and heal.
37. Cover yourself with the blood of Jesus.

38. I hold the blood of Jesus, as a shield against any power that is already poised to resist me, in the name of Jesus.
39. By the blood of Jesus, I stand against every device of distractions, in the name of Jesus.
40. I stand upon the word of God and I declare myself unmoveable, in the name of Jesus.
41. Father Lord let me be strengthened with might by Your Spirit my the inner man, in the name of Jesus.
42. Blood of Jesus purge my tabernacle, in Jesus name.
43. Father Lord, let my body soul and spirit be preserved blameless unto the coming of our Lord Jesus Christ, in the name of Jesus.
44. Every yoke manufacturer, arise, carry your yoke and die, in Jesus name.
45. I release myself, from every ancestral demonic pollution, in Jesus name.
46. I release myself from any inherited bondage and limitation, in the name of Jesus.
47. O Lord, send Your axe of fire to the foundation of my life, and destroy every evil plantation therein.
48. Holy Ghost fire, pass through my life, purge my spirit, soul and body.
49. Power of pollution dominating my life, die, in Jesus.
50. Blood of Jesus flush out from my system, every inherited satanic deposit, in the name of Jesus.
51. Lord Jesus, cleanse my spirit, soul, and body from all filthiness.

52. I cut myself off from every spirit of . . . (mention the name of your place of birth), in the name of Jesus.
53. I uproot, (pick from the under listed) from the foundation of my life, in the name of Jesus.

- Poison of darkness
- Ancestral initiation
- Negative programming
- Poverty
- Triangular trap
- Bewitchment power
- Idol deposit
- Sexual pollution
- Witchcraft hatred

54. You evil foundational plantation, come out of my life with all your roots, in the name of Jesus! (*Lay your hands on your stomach and keep repeating the emphasized area.*)
55. I release myself from demonic pollution, emanating from my parents' religion in the name of Jesus.
56. I release myself from demonic pollution, emanating from my past involvement in any demonic religion, in the name of Jesus.
57. I break and loose myself from every idol and related association, in Jesus name.
58. I release myself, from every dream pollution, in Jesus name.

59. I break and loose myself from every form of demonic bewitchment, in the name of Jesus.
60. I release myself from every evil domination and control, in the name of Jesus.
61. Every gate, opened to the enemy by my foundation, be closed forever with the blood of Jesus.
62. I release myself from the grip of any problem transferred into my life from the womb, in the name of Jesus.
63. I break and loose myself from every inherited evil curse, in the name of Jesus.
64. I vomit every evil consumption, that I have been fed as a child, in the name of Jesus.
65. I command all foundational strongmen attached to my life to be paralysed, in the name of Jesus.
66. Evil strangers in my body, come all the way out of your hiding places, in the name of Jesus.
67. I disconnect any conscious or unconscious link with demonic caterers, in the name of Jesus.
68. O Lord, let all avenues to eat or drink spiritual poisons be closed in the name of Jesus.
69. Dream defilement over my life, die in Jesus name.
70. I cough out and vomit any food eaten from the table of the devil, in the name of Jesus. (*Cough them out and vomit them in faith. Prime the expulsion.*)

71. All negative materials circulating in my blood stream, come out and catch fire, in the name of Jesus.
72. I drink the blood of Jesus. (*Physically swallow and drink it in faith. Keep doing this for some time.*)
73. (*Lay one hand on your head and the other on your stomach or navel and begin to pray like this*) Holy Ghost fire, burn from the top of my head to the sole of my feet. (*Begin to mention every organ of your body; your kidney, liver, intestines, blood, etc. You must not rush at this level, because the fire will actually come and you may start feeling the heat.*)
74. Blood of Jesus and the fire of the Holy Ghost, cleanse every organ in my body, in the name of Jesus.
75. Every astral projection into my body . . . (head, chest, stomach, womb), I bind you and cast you out, in the name of Jesus.
76. My head, reject the landing space for darkness, in the name of Jesus.
77. Ladders of darkness, permitting evil infiltration into my life, scatter in the name of Jesus.
78. Programme of the enemy for my body, I disapprove you now, in the name of Jesus.
79. I cancel every spell, enchantment and divination assigned against me, in the name of Jesus.
80. Dark strangers release my life, in the name of Jesus.
81. Every unwelcome visitor in the habitation of my life, get out now, in the name of Jesus.

82. Holy Spirit, purge me from any evil mark put upon me, in the name of Jesus.
83. O Lord, let the blood of Jesus be transfused into my blood vessel.
84. My body, soul and spirit reject evil load in Jesus' name.
85. Every inherited sickness in my life, depart from me now, in the name of Jesus
86. Evil water in my body, get out, in the name of Jesus.
87. Evil foundation in my life, I pull you down today in the mighty name of Jesus.
88. Holy Ghost fire, immunize my blood against satanic poisoning in the name of Jesus.
89. Let God be God in my health.
90. Lord Jesus, walk back into every second of my life and deliver me where I need deliverance; heal me where I need healing and transform me where I need transformation.
91. I release my body system from the cage of every household wickedness. In the name of Jesus.
92. Let every information about my body systems be erased from every satanic memory in the name of Jesus.
93. O Lord, create in me a clean heart by your power.
94. O Lord let the anointing of the Holy Spirit break every yoke of backwardness in my life.
95. Thou brush of the Lord scrub out every dirtiness in my spiritual pipe, in the name of Jesus.
96. O Lord establish me as a holy person unto You.

97. Let my spirit man become divine fire.
98. I frustrate every demonic arrest over my spirit man, in Jesus name.
99. O Lord let the anointing to excel in my spiritual and physical life fall upon me.
100. O Lord produce in me the power of self control and gentleness.
101. Holy Ghost fire, ignite me to the glory of God.
102. I command every spiritual contamination in my life to receive cleansing by the blood of Jesus.
103. Heavenly surgeon visit me now, in the name of Jesus.
104. Every handwriting of darkness targeted against my health, be wiped off in the name of Jesus.
105. Every rusted spiritual pipe in my life, receive wholeness, in the name of Jesus.
106. I command every power, eating up my spiritual pipe to be roasted, in the name of Jesus.
107. I renounce any evil dedication placed upon my life, in the name of Jesus.
108. I break every evil edict and ordination, in Jesus' name.
109. O Lord, cleanse all the soiled parts of my life.
110. Let every evil effect of any strange touches be removed from my life, in the name of Jesus.
111. O Lord, heal every wounded part of my life.
112. You strongman of body destruction, be bound, in Jesus name.

113. You strongman of mind destruction, be bound, in Jesus' name.

114. Distributor of spiritual poison, swallow your poison, in Jesus name.

115. O Lord, bend every evil rigidity of my life.

116. O Lord re-align every satanic straying in my life.

117. O Lord let the fire of the Holy Spirit warm every satanic freeze in my life.

118. O Lord, give me a life that kills death

119. O Lord, kindle in me the fire of charity.

120. O Lord, glue me together where I am opposed to myself.

121. O Lord, enrich me with Your gifts.

122. O Lord, quicken me and increase my desire for the things of heaven.

123. By your rulership, O Lord, let the lust of the flesh in my life die.

124. O Lord, refine and purge my life, by Your fire.

125. Lord Jesus, increase daily in my life and maintain Your gifts in me.

126. I claim my complete deliverance from the spirit of . . . (mention those things you do not desire in your life), in Jesus name.

127. Let the water of life flush out every unwanted stranger in my life, in the name of Jesus.

128. Let every Achan depart from my camp, in the name of Jesus.
129. Holy Spirit, help me to locate the defect in the clay of my life.
130. O Lord, remove from my life anything that will make me to miss the rapture.
131. I declare myself a virgin for the Lord, in the name of Jesus.
132. Lord, make me the voice of deliverance and blessings.
133. I seal my victory with the blood of Jesus.
134. Lord Jesus I thank you for answered prayers.

Prayer Section

Four

SATANIC OPPRESSORS, LET ME GO!

INTRODUCTION:
These prayers are for you to deal with those powers that have determined that you will not sing your song and dance your dance over your marriage and every other facet of your life. If you have been dejected, depressed and discouraged, if you. think all hope has been lost, do not give up. Encourage yourself in the Lord just as David did, take these prayer points with holy aggression, violent faith and stubborn determination and your miracles shall appear, in the name of Jesus.

Confession: Psalm 68:1: *"Let God arise, let his enemies be scattered: let them also that hate him flee before him."*

Praise Worship

Prayer Points

1. O wind of God, drive away every power of the ungodly rising against my destiny, in the name of Jesus.
2. Let the rage of the wicked against me be rendered impotent, in the name of Jesus.
3. Let the imagination of the wicked against me be neutralized, in the name of Jesus.

4. Every counsel of evil kings against me, be scattered, in the name of Jesus.

5. O God, arise and speak in great wrath against the enemy of my breakthroughs, in the name of Jesus.

6. Every band of the wicked that is arresting my progress, break, in the name of Jesus.

7. Every cord of darkness militating against my breakthroughs, die, in the name of Jesus.

8. O God, arise and laugh my enemies to scorn, in Jesus' name.

9. O God, arise and speak unto my enemies in Your wrath, in the name of Jesus.

10. O God, vex my stubborn oppressors in Your sore displeasure, in the name of Jesus.

11. O Lord, break my enemies with Your rod of iron, in Jesus' name.

12. O God, dash the power of stubborn pursuers in pieces like a potter's vessel, in the name of Jesus.

13. O God, arise with all Your weapons of war and fight my battle for me, in the name of Jesus.

14. O God, be my glory and the lifter of my head, in Jesus' name.

15. My Father, be a shield for me in every situation, in Jesus' name.

16. O God, hear my cry out of Your holy hill, in the name of Jesus.
17. I will not be afraid of ten thousands of people that have set themselves against me, in the name of Jesus.
18. O God, smite my enemies by the cheekbones, in Jesus' name.
19. My Father, break the teeth of the ungodly, in Jesus' name.
20. O Lord, hear my voice whenever I call, in the name of Jesus.
21. O God, visit every power lying against me with destruction, in the name of Jesus.
22. Lead me, O Lord, in Thy righteousness, in the name of Jesus.
23. O Lord, make Your way plain before my face, in Jesus' name.
24. Let my enemies fall by their own counsel, in the name of Jesus.
25. Cast out my enemies in the multitude of their transgressions, in the name of Jesus.
26. Every organized worker of iniquity, depart from me, in the name of Jesus.
27. Let all my enemies be ashamed and sore vexed, in Jesus' name.
28. Let sudden shame be the lot of all my oppressors, in Jesus' name
29. Every power planning to tear my soul like a lion, be dismantled, in the name of Jesus.

30. O God, command judgment on all my oppressors, in Jesus' name.
31. Let the wickedness of the wicked come to an end, O Lord, in the name of Jesus.
32. O Lord, let Your anger boil against the wicked every day, in the name of Jesus.
33. O God, prepare the instruments of death against my enemies, in the name of Jesus.
34. O God, ordain Your arrows against my persecutors, in the name of Jesus.
35. Let every pit dug by the enemy become a grave for the enemy, in the name of Jesus.
36. Let the mischief of my enemies return upon his own head, in the name of Jesus.
37. Let all weapons of my enemies backfire by thunder, in the name of Jesus.
38. O God, ordain strength for me and still the enemy and the avenger, in the name of Jesus.
39. When mine enemies are turned back, they shall perish out of Thy presence, in the name of Jesus.
40. O God, destroy the wicked and put out their name forever and ever, in the name of Jesus.
41. Let the enemy sink in the pit they have made, in Jesus' name.
42. Let the feet of the enemy be taken in the net which he hid, in the name of Jesus.

43. Let the wicked be snared in the work of his own hands, in the name of Jesus.
44. Arise O Lord, let not man prevail, let the heathen be judged in Thy sight, in the name of Jesus.
45. Put the enemies in fear, O Lord, that the nations may know themselves to be but men, in the name of Jesus.
46. Let the wicked be taken in the devices they have imagined, in the name of Jesus.
47. Arise O Lord, lift up Thine arm in war, in the name of Jesus.
48. Break Thou the arm of the wicked and the evil man, in the name of Jesus.
49. Upon the wicked O Lord, rain snares, fire and brimstone and a horrible tempest, in the name of Jesus.
50. My enemies shall not rejoice over me, in the name of Jesus.
51. Keep me as the apple of Thy eye, hide me under the shadow of Thy wings, O Lord, in the name of Jesus.
52. Barricade me from the wicked that oppress me and from my deadly enemies who compass me about, in the name of Jesus.
53. Arise O Lord, disappoint my oppressors and cast them down, in the name of Jesus.
54. O Lord, deliver my soul from the wicked which is Thy sword, in the name of Jesus.
55. I will call upon the Lord, who is worthy to be praised, so shall I be saved from mine enemies, in Jesus' name.

56. O God send out Your arrows and scatter the oppressors, in the name of Jesus.
57. O God, shoot out Your lightening and discomfit them, in the name of Jesus.
58. Let the smoke go out of Your nostrils and fire out of Your mouth to devour all plantations of darkness in my life, in Jesus' name
59. O God, thunder from heaven against all my oppressors, in the name of Jesus.
60. O Lord, at the blast of Your nostrils, disgrace every foundational bondage, in the name of Jesus.
61. O God, deliver me from my strong enemy which hated me for they are too strong for me, in Jesus' name.
62. O God, bring down every high look that is downgrading my potentials, in the name of Jesus.
63. I receive power to run through satanic troops, in Jesus' name.
64. I receive power to leap over every demonic wall of barrier, in the name of Jesus.
65. O Lord, teach my hands to war, in the name of Jesus.
66. Let every bow of steel fashioned by the enemy be broken by my hands, in the name of Jesus.
67. I receive the power to pursue and overtake my enemies, in the name of Jesus.
68. My enemies are wounded, they are unable to rise, they are fallen under my feet, in the name of Jesus.

69. O God, subdue under me those that rose up against me, in the name of Jesus.
70. O God, arise and give me the neck of my enemies, that I might destroy them that hate me, in Jesus' name..
71. My enemies will cry, but there will be none to deliver them, in the name of Jesus.
72. I receive power to beat my aggressors to smallness as the dust before the wind, in the name of Jesus.
73. I cast out my pursuers as the dirt in the street, in Jesus' name.
74. By Your favour, O Lord, the people whom I have not known shall serve me, in the name of Jesus.
75. As soon as they hear of me, they shall obey me, the strangers shall submit themselves unto me, in the name of Jesus.
76. The dark strangers in my life shall fade away and be afraid out of their close places, in the name of Jesus.
77. O God, avenge me and subdue my adversaries under me, in the name of Jesus.
78. The Lord shall hear me in the day of trouble, the name of the God of Jacob shall defend me, in the name of Jesus.
79. O Lord, send me help from Your sanctuary and strengthen me out of Zion, in the name of Jesus.
80. My adversaries are brought down and fallen but I rise and stand upright, in the name of Jesus.

81. Let Thine hand find out all Thine enemies, let Thy right hand find out those that hate Thee, in Jesus' name.
82. O God, make my adversaries as a fiery oven in the time of Thine anger, in the name of Jesus.
83. O God, arise and swallow up my enemies in Your wrath and let Your fire devour them, in the name of Jesus.
84. Let every seed and fruit of the enemy fashioned against my destiny be destroyed, in the name of Jesus.
85. Let the mischievous device of the enemy backfire, in the name of Jesus.
86. O God, arise and make all my pursuers turn back, in Jesus' name.
87. O Lord, let Your arrows pursue and locate every wicked power targeted against me, in the name of Jesus.
88. Do not be far from me, O Lord, be my help in the time of trouble, in the name of Jesus.
89. O Lord, make haste to help me, in the name of Jesus.
90. O Lord, deliver my soul from the sword and my destiny from the power of the dog, in the name of Jesus.
91. O God, arise by the thunder of Your power and save me from the lion's mouth, in the name of Jesus.
92. Thou power of the valley of the shadow of death, release my destiny, in the name of Jesus.
94. O gates blocking my blessings, be lifted up, in Jesus' name.
95. O Lord, keep my soul, let me not be ashamed and deliver me, in the name of Jesus.

Prayer Section

Five

SATANIC OPPRESSORS, LET ME GO!
(PART 2)

INTRODUCTION

The importance of having a second section for this particular prayer heading is its necessity to the achievement of your dominion in the real sense of it. So take it with strong determination and seriousness, and I am sure that the great God will rent the heavens apart for your sake, in the name of Jesus.

CONFESSION: Is. 49:25-26 "But thus saith the Lord, Even the captives of the mighty shall be taken away, and the prey of the terrible shall be delivered: for I will contend with him that contendeth with thee, and I will save thy children. And I will feed them that oppress thee with their own flesh; and they shall be drunken with their own blood, as with sweet wine: and all flesh shall know that I the Lord am thy Saviour and thy Redeemer, the mighty One of Jacob."

PRAISE WORSHIP

PRAYER POINTS

1. Every drinker of blood and eater of flesh coming against me, die, in the name of Jesus.
2. Though an host should encamp against me, my heart shall not fear, in the name of Jesus.
3. Though war should rise against me, in this will I be confident, in the name of Jesus.
4. And now shall my head be lifted up above my enemies round about me, in the name of Jesus.
5. Deliver me not over unto the will of mine enemies, in the name of Jesus.
6. God shall destroy the camp of the enemy and their camp shall never be built up, in the name of Jesus.
7. O Lord, according to the deeds of the wicked, give them the works of their hands, in the name of Jesus.
8. O Lord, put off my sack cloth and gird me with gladness, in the name of Jesus.
9. Bow down Thine ear to me, O Lord, and deliver me speedily, in the name of Jesus.
10. Pull me out of the hidden net of the enemy, in Jesus' name.
11. My times are in Thy hand, deliver me from the hands of mine enemies and from that persecute me, in the name of Jesus.

12. Let the wicked be ashamed and let them be silent in the grave, in the name of Jesus.
13. Every lying lip speaking against me, be silenced, in Jesus' name.
14. O Lord, bring the counsel of the ungodly to naught, in the name of Jesus.
15. Many sorrows shall be to the wicked, in the name of Jesus.
16. O Lord, make the devices of my adversaries of none effect, in the name of Jesus.
17. Evil shall slay the wicked and they that hate the righteous shall be desolate, in the name of Jesus.
18. Father, fight against them that fight against me, in the name of Jesus.
19. Father, take hold of my shield and buckler and stand up for mine help.
20. Father, draw out Your spear and stop my persecutors, in Jesus' name.
21. Let them be confounded and put to shame that seek after my soul, in the name of Jesus.
22. Let them be turned back and brought to confusion that device my hurt, in the name of Jesus.
23. Let the wicked be as chaff before the wind and let the anger of the Lord chase them, in the name of Jesus.
24. Let the way of the oppressor be dark and slippery and let the angel of the Lord persecute them, in the name of Jesus.

25. Let destruction come upon my enemies unawares and the net that he hath hid catch himself, in Jesus' name.
26. Let the enemy fall into the destruction he has created, in the name of Jesus.
27. Let not them that are mine enemies wrongfully rejoice over me, in the name of Jesus.
28. Let my enemies be ashamed and brought to confusion together with them that rejoice at mine hurt, in the name of Jesus.
29. Let my enemies be clothed with shame, in the name of Jesus.
30. Stir up thyself, O Lord, and fight for me, in Jesus' name.
31. Let them be clothed with shame and dishonour that magnify themselves against me, in the name of Jesus.
32. Let not the foot of pride come against me, in Jesus' name.
33. Let not the hand of the wicked prosper in my life, in the name of Jesus.
34. Every worker of death, be cast down and be unable to rise, in the name of Jesus.
35. O God, arise and laugh at the plot of the wicked fashioned against me, in the name of Jesus.
36. Let their sword enter into their own heart and let their bows be broken, in the name of Jesus.
37. Let the arms of the wicked be broken, in the name of Jesus.
38. My enemies shall be as the fat of lambs, they shall be consumed and into smoke shall they be consumed away, in the name of Jesus.

39. Let them be desolate that laugh me to scorn, in Jesus' name.
40. Every enemy saying where is my God, be disgraced, in the name of Jesus.
41. Through Thee I will push down my enemies, through Thy name I will tread them under them that rise up against me, in Jesus' name.
42. O Lord, break the slip of my Goliath with Your east wind, in the name of Jesus.
43. Let death feed upon every witchcraft power, in Jesus' name.
44. O Lord, redeem my soul from the power of the grave, in the name of Jesus.
45. I will call upon the Lord in the day of trouble and He shall deliver me, in the name of Jesus.
46. Lord, reward evil unto mine enemies and cut them off in Thy truth, in the name of Jesus.
47. Destroy, O Lord, and divide every power conspiring against my destiny, in the name of Jesus.
48. Every power of the night working against my victory, die, in the name of Jesus.
49. O Lord, let death seize upon them and let them go down quick to hell that devise disgrace against me, in the name of Jesus.
50. O God, arise and afflict my affliction, in the name of Jesus.
51. When I cry unto Thee then shall mine enemies turn back, this I know, for God is for me, in the name of Jesus.

52. O God, break the teeth of the evil lion targeted against me, in the name of Jesus.
53. Let my oppressors melt away as waters which run continuously, in the name of Jesus.
54. Let Your whirlwind blow away every oppression, in Jesus' name.
55. Deliver me from the workers of iniquity and save me from bloody men, in the name of Jesus.
56. Every power of the dog working late at night against me, be dismantled, in the name of Jesus.
57. God shall let me see my desire upon my enemies, in the name of Jesus.
58. Scatter by Your power, O Lord, them that devise my fall, in the name of Jesus.
59. Let my enemies be taken in their pride, in the name of Jesus.
60. Give me help from troubles for vain is the help of man, in the name of Jesus.
61. Through God, I shall do valiantly, for He is that shall tread down my enemies, in the name of Jesus.
62. Those that seek my soul to destroy it shall go down into the lower parts of the earth, in the name of Jesus.
63. My problem shall fall by the sword and shall be a portion for foxes, in the name of Jesus.
64. Hear my voice, O God, preserve me from the fear of the enemy, in the name of Jesus.

65. Hide me, O God, from the secret counsel of the wicked, in the name of Jesus.
66. O God, shoot at my enemies with an arrow, suddenly shall they be wounded, in the name of Jesus.
67. The tongue of my adversaries shall fall upon them and all that see them shall flee away, in the name of Jesus.
68. Let God arise and let all His enemies be scattered, let them that hate Him flee before Him, in the name of Jesus.
69. As smoke is driven away, so drive away the hand of the oppressor, in the name of Jesus.
70. Let every power rebelling against my breakthroughs be made to dwell in a dry land, in the name of Jesus.
71. O God, wound the heart of all my stubborn pursuers, in the name of Jesus.
72. O Lord, rebuke the company of darkness and scatter them, in the name of Jesus.
73. Let the table of my enemies become a snare before them and that which should have been for their welfare, let it become a trap, in the name of Jesus.
74. Pour out Thine indignation upon the enemies of my soul, in the name of Jesus.
75. Let their habitation or house become desolate and let none dwell in their tents, in the name of Jesus.
76. Let those that seek my soul be turned back and put to confusion, in the name of Jesus.

77. Let them be confounded and consumed that are adversaries of my soul, in the name of Jesus.
78. All my enemies shall lick the dust, in the name of Jesus.
79. O God, break the head of the dragon in the water, in the name of Jesus.
80. O God, break the head of Leviathan in pieces, in Jesus' name.
81. Arise, O God, plead Thine own cause, remember how the foolish man reproacheth Thee daily, in the name of Jesus.
82. All the horns of the wicked also shall be cut off, in the name of Jesus.
83. At Thy rebuke, O God of Jacob, both the chariot and the horse are cast into a dead sleep, in the name of Jesus.
84. Let the wrath of the enemy against me be converted to testimonies, in the name of Jesus.
85. O Lord, send evil angels after the enemies of my soul, in the name of Jesus.
86. O God, smite the enemies in their hinder parts and put them to a perpetual reproach, in the name of Jesus.
87. O Lord, feed my enemies with the bread of tears and give them tears to drink in great measure, in the name of Jesus.
88. Let the stars fight against my enemies after the order of Sisera, in the name of Jesus.
89. O God, make my enemies like a wheel, as the stubble before the wind, in the name of Jesus.

90. Persecute my enemies with Thy tempest and make them afraid with Thy storm, in the name of Jesus.
91. Fill the faces of my aggressors with shame that they may seek thy name, O Lord, in the name of Jesus.
92. Let my enemies be confounded and troubled, in Jesus' name.
93. Every assembly of the violent men, be scattered, in the name of Jesus.
94. O Lord, break down the hedges of the wicked and bring their strongholds to ruin, in the name of Jesus.
95. I shall not be afraid for the terror by night, nor for the arrow that flieth by day, in the name of Jesus.
96. A thousand shall fall at my side and ten thousand at my right hand, but it shall not come near me, in the name of Jesus.
97. Mine eyes shall see my desires on mine enemies, in Jesus' name
98. Let fire go before me and burn up my enemies round about, in the name of Jesus.
99. At Thy rebuke, let Thine enemies flee, at the voice of Thy thunder, let them hasten away, in the name of Jesus.
100. Thou power that troubled the Egyptians, trouble my enemies, in the name of Jesus.
101. O gates of brass and bars of iron working against me, be broken, in the name of Jesus.

102. Let the rivers of my enemies be turned into wilderness, in the name of Jesus.
103. Set a wicked man over the wicked, in the name of Jesus.
104. Let the days of my enemies be cut off and let another take his office, in the name of Jesus.
105. As the enemy loves cursing, let it come unto him, in the name of Jesus.
106. As the enemy delights not in blessings, so let it be far from him, in the name of Jesus.
107. As the enemy clothes himself with cursing like as with his garment, so let it come into his bowels like water and like oil into his bones, in the name of Jesus.
108. The wicked shall be grieved and his desire shall perish, in the name of Jesus.
109. I come against every form of barrenness in my life, in the name of Jesus.
110. Let all those who consult darkness against me be disgraced, in the name of Jesus.
111. The Lord is on my side, I will not fear what can man do unto me, in the name of Jesus.
112. Depart from me ye evil doers, for I will keep the commandments of my God, in the name of Jesus.
113. Deliver me from the oppression of man, in the name of Jesus.
114. O righteous God, cut off the cords of the wicked, in the name of Jesus.
115. Let them be confounded and turned back that hate Zion, in the name of Jesus.
116. Let the wicked be as the grass upon the house tops which withers afore it grows up, in the name of Jesus.

Prayer Section

Six

Marital Dominion (PART ONE)

INTRODUCTION

This prayer heading is for those to whom sharing the testimony of marriage has now become like a mirage. All suitors who come your way either have one issue or the other that prevent your successful marriage or perhaps none is even coming your way. It is time for you to claim with aggressive faith the glorious home that God has designed for you. As you pray these prayers, your marital heavens will open, in the name of Jesus.

CONFESSION: Phil.2:9, Col.2:13, Rev.12:12, Luke 1:37

Daniel 2:22 *'He revealeth the deep and secret things: he knoweth what is in the darkness, and the light dwelleth with him.*

PRAISE WORSHIP

PRAYER

1. Thank the Lord because this year is your year of dumbfounding miracles.
2. Confess these scriptures out loud: Philippians 2:9; Colossians 2:13; Rev. 12:12; Luke 1:37.
3. Lord, make known to me the secrets needed for my marital breakthrough.
4. Help me Lord, to discover my real self.
5. Let every imagination of the enemy against my marital life be rendered impotent in the name of Jesus.
6. I refuse to co-operate with any anti-marriage spells and curses in the name of Jesus.
7. I cancel every bewitchment fashioned against my settling down in marriage in the name of Jesus.
8. Let every force magnetizing the wrong people to me be paralysed in the name of Jesus.
9. I break every covenant of marital failure and late marriage in the name of Jesus.
10. I cancel every spiritual wedding conducted consciously or unconsciously on my behalf in Jesus' name.
11. I remove the hand of household wickedness from my marital life in the name of Jesus.

12. Let every incantation, incision, hex and other spiritually harmful activities working against my marriage, be completely neutralized in the name of Jesus.
13. I command all forces of evil manipulating, delaying or hindering my marriage to be completely paralysed in the name of Jesus.
14. Let all evil anti-marriage covenants be broken in the name of Jesus.
15. Lord, restore me to the perfect way in which You created me if I have been altered.
16. Father, let Your fire destroy every satanic weapon fashioned against my marriage in the name of Jesus.
17. I forsake any personal sin that has given ground to the enemy in the name of Jesus.
18. I reclaim all the ground I have lost to the enemy in the name of Jesus.
19. Let the blood of Jesus speak against every power working against my marriage.
20. I apply the blood of Jesus to remove all consequences of evil operations and oppression in Jesus' name
21. I break the binding effect of anything of evil ever put upon me from any source in the name of Jesus.
22. I remove the right of the enemy to afflict my plan to get married in the name of Jesus.
23. I break every bondage of inherited marital confusion in the name of Jesus.

24. I bind and plunder the goods of every strongman plans attached to my marriage in the name of Jesus.
25. Let the Angels of the living God roll away the stone blocking my marital breakthroughs in Jesus' name.
26. Let God arise and let all the enemies of my marital breakthrough be scattered in the name of Jesus.
27. Let the Fire of God melt away the stones hindering my marital blessings in the mighty name of Jesus.
28. Let the cloud blocking the sunlight of my marital breakthrough be dispersed in Jesus' name.
29. Let all evil spirits masquerading to trouble my marital life, be bound in the name of Jesus.
30. Lord, let wonderful changes be my lot this year.
31. Lord, turn away all that would jilt, disappoint or fail me in the name of Jesus.
32. Every secret, covenant and vow affecting my destiny, be broken, in the name of Jesus.
33. Every ancestral secret retarding my progress, be revealed, in the name of Jesus.
34. Evil secret activities currently affecting my life, be exposed and disgraced, in the name of Jesus.
35. Every secret I need to know to excel spiritually and financially, be revealed, in the name of Jesus.
36. Every secret hidden in the marine kingdom, affecting my elevation, be exposed and disgraced, in Jesus' name.
37. Every secret hidden in the satanic archive, crippling my elevation, be exposed and disgraced, in Jesus' name.

38. Every secret I need to know about my environment, be revealed, in the name of Jesus.
39. Secrets of wicked elders behind my challenges, be exposed and disgraced, in the name of Jesus.
40. Every secret I need to know about my father's lineage, be revealed, in the name of Jesus.
41. Every secret I need to know about my mother's lineage, be revealed, in the name of Jesus.
42. Every secret I need to know about my hometown, be revealed, in the name of Jesus. .
43. Every secret I need to know about the work I am doing, be revealed, in the name of Jesus.
44. Every power that wants my efforts to turn against me, I pull you down, in the name of Jesus.
45. O Lord, lift evil stones away from my body, in the name of Jesus.
46. O God, arise and stir the winds to bring me restoration, in the name of Jesus.
47. O Lord, call forth new patterns in my life that will promote me, in the name of Jesus.
48. Evil winds blowing against me, be reversed, in the name of Jesus.
49. Afflictions, hear the word of the Lord, become promotions, in the name of Jesus.
50. Let my glory be perfected by fire, in the name of Jesus.

51. Blood of Jesus, stand between me and every strange altar, in the name of Jesus.
52. Blood of Jesus, secure my portion, secure and my destiny, in the name of Jesus.
53. Blood of Jesus, walk through my family and scatter every witchcraft operation, in the name of Jesus.
54. Blood of Jesus, open up all gates shut against me, in the name of Jesus.
55. O God, restore the structure of my life in the perfection in which You ordained it, in the name of Jesus.
56. O God, rebuild the damaged walls of my life, in the name of Jesus.
57. Every strange altar of fear, scatter, in the name of Jesus.
58. I destroy every covenant of fear by the blood of the Lamb.
59. You dead works in my life, get out now, in the name of Jesus.
60. Every secret agenda of _ _ _ (pick from the following lists), assigned against my life, scatter, in Jesus' name.
    - star hijacker
    - destiny killer
    - territorial demotion
    - gate of evil
    - placental manipulation
    - poverty activator
    - coffin spirit
    - evil bullet
    - wicked broadcaster
    - children killer
    - evil reinforcement
    - pocket with holes
    - desert spirit
    - iron-like curses
    - head manipulator
    - satanic poison
    - arrow of fruitless efforts
    - unfriendly friend
    - evil observer
    - vagabond anointing
    - dark agent
    - business bewitchment
    - arrow of infirmity
    - evil mark
    - evil spirit marriage
    - progress arrester
    - spirit of tragedy
    - strange money
    - rain of affliction
    - witchcraft handwriting
    - marriage killer
    - spirit of death and hell

61. O Lord, give unto me the Spirit of revelation and wisdom in the knowledge of Yourself.
62. O Lord, make Your way plain before my face on this issue.
63. O Lord, remove spiritual cataract from my eyes.
64. O Lord, forgive me for every false motive or thought that has ever been formed in my heart since the day I was born.
65. O Lord, forgive me for any lie that I have ever told against any person, system or organization.
66. O Lord, deliver me from the bondage and sin of spiritual laziness.
67. O Lord, open up my eyes to see all I should see on my marital issue.
68. O Lord, teach me deep and secret things.
69. O Lord, reveal to me every secret behind any problem that I have.
70. O Lord, bring to the light everything planned against me in darkness.
71. O Lord, ignite and revive my beneficial potentials.
72. O Lord, give me divine wisdom to operate my life.
73. O Lord, let every veil preventing me from having plain spiritual vision be removed.
74. O Lord, give unto me the spirit of revelation and wisdom in the knowledge of You.
75. O Lord, open up my spiritual understanding.
76. O Lord, let me know all I should know about this issue.
77. O Lord, reveal to me every secret behind the particular issue whether beneficial or not.

78. O Lord, remove from me any persistent buried grudges, half-acknowledged enmity against anyone and every other thing that can block my spiritual vision.
79. O Lord, teach me to know that which is worth knowing and love that which is worth loving and to dislike whatsoever is not pleasing to Your eyes.
80. O Lord, make me a vessel capable of knowing Your secret things.
81. Father in the name of Jesus, I ask to know Your mind about ... (slot in the appropriate situation) situation.
82. Let the spirit of prophesy and revelation fall upon the totality of my being, in the name of Jesus.
83. Holy Spirit, reveal deep and the secret things to me about. .., in the name of Jesus.
84. I bind every demon that pollutes spiritual vision and dreams, in the name of Jesus.
85. Let every dirtiness blocking my communication pipe with the living God be washed clean with the blood of Jesus, in the name of Jesus.
86. I receive power to operate with sharp spiritual eyes that cannot be deceived, in the name of Jesus.
87. Let the glory and the power of the Almighty God, fall upon my life in a mighty way, in the name of Jesus.
88. I remove my name from the book of those who grope and stumble in darkness, in the name of Jesus.
89. Divine revelations, spiritual visions, dreams and information will not become scarce commodity in my life, in the name of Jesus.

90. I drink to the full in the well of salvation and anointing, in the name of Jesus.
91. O God, to whom no secret is hidden, make know unto me whether . . . (mention the name of the thing) is Your choice for me, in the name of Jesus.
92. Let every idol present consciously or unconsciously in my heart concerning this issue be melted away by the fire of the Holy Spirit, in the name of Jesus.
93. I refuse to fall under the manipulation of the spirits of confusion, in the name of Jesus.
94. I refuse to make foundational mistakes in my decision making, in the name of Jesus.
95. Father Lord, guide and direct me in knowing Your mind on this particular issue, in the name of Jesus.
96. I stand against all satanic attachments that may seek to confuse my decision, in the name of Jesus.
97. If . . . (mention the name of the thing) is not for me, O Lord, redirect my steps.
98. I bind the activities of . . . (pick from the list below) in my life, in the name of Jesus.
    (i)   lust   (ii)   ungodly infatuation
    (iii) ungodly family pressure
    (iv) demonic manipulation in dreams and visions
    (v) attachment from/to the wrong choice (vi) c o n f u s i n g revelations

(vii) spiritual blindness and deafness

(viii) unprofitable advice

(ix) ungodly impatience

99. O God, You who reveals secret things, make known unto me Your choice for me in this issue, in Jesus' name.

100. Holy Spirit, open my eyes and help me to make the right decision, in the name of Jesus.

101. Thank You Jesus for Your presence and the good testimonies that will follow.

102. Pray in the spirit, if you have received the baptism of the Holy Spirit, for at least 15 minutes before going to bed.

Prayer Section

Seven

MARITAL DOMINION (PART 2)

INTRODUCTION
These are prayers that will ensure that your marital breakthrough manifests. As you pray these prayers, any power standing on the way of your marriage will be cleared away by the bulldozing power of the Holy Ghost, in the name of Jesus.

Confession - Genesis 24:1-33

Praise worship

Prayer Points
1. Lord Jesus, begin to organize the programme of my rightful spouse for my speedy marriage and re-organize my programme for speedy marriage, in the name of Jesus.
2. Let everything in the surrounding of my rightful spouse begin to speak for my favour in marriage, in the name of Jesus.
3. I command everything in the surrounding of me and my spouse to speak for my favour in marriage, in the name of Jesus.
4. O Lord, lift up divine intercessors for my marriage, in the name of Jesus.
5. Oh Lord, programme my spouse to locate me in my closet, in the name of Jesus.

6. I cast out every spirit of error and confusion against my marriage, in the name of Jesus.
7. I command the household of my rightful spouse not to agree with any stranger as my replacement, in the name of Jesus.
8. Oh Lord God of heaven and earth, let all things that you created be ruled by Your angels to work together for my success in marriage, in the name of Jesus.
9. I shall not work against my divine purpose in marriage, in the name of Jesus.
10. Oh Lord, open Your heavens and rain blessings upon me and my spouse for our marriage to be successful, in the name of Jesus.
11. I refuse for my rightful spouse to tarry at satanic bus stop before locating me, in the name of Jesus.
12. Oh Lord, increase the thirst of my spouse towards me, in the name of Jesus.
13. Oh Lord, hasty my footsteps towards my identifying my rightful spouse and open the eyes of my rightful spouse to identify me, in the name of Jesus.
14. Lord Jesus, open my eyes to identify my rightful spouse and open the eyes of my rightful spouse to identify me, in the name of Jesus.
15. Lord Jesus, cause me to speak the rightful word that will lead to my breakthrough in marriage, in the name of Jesus.
16. O Lord, cause me to act favorably towards my breakthrough in marriage, in the name of Jesus.

17. Lord Jesus, order my footsteps into rightful marriage, in the name of Jesus.
18. O Lord, give my spouse and myself Your divine words in our marriage, in the name of Jesus.
19. Lord, make known to me the secrets needed for my marital breakthrough.
20. Help me Lord, to discover my real self.
21. Let every imagination of the enemy against my marital life be rendered impotent in the name of Jesus.
22. I refuse to co-operate with any anti-marriage spells and curses in the name of Jesus.
23. I cancel every bewitchment fashioned against my settling down in marriage in the name of Jesus.
24. Let every force magnetizing the wrong people to me be paralysed in the name of Jesus.
25. I break every covenant of marital failure and late marriage in the name of Jesus.
26. I cancel every spiritual wedding conducted consciously or unconsciously on my behalf in Jesus' name.
27. I remove the hand of household wickedness from my marital life in the name of Jesus.
28. Let every incantation, incisions, hexes and other spiritually harmful activities working against my marriage, be completely neutralized in the name of Jesus.
29. I command all forces of evil manipulating, delaying or hindering my marriage to be completely paralysed in the name of Jesus.

30. Let all evil anti-marriage covenants be broken in the name of Jesus.
31. Lord, restore me to the perfect way in which You created me if I have been altered.
32. Father, let Your fire destroy every satanic weapon fashioned against my marriage in the name of Jesus.
33. I forsake any personal sin that has given ground to the enemy in the name of Jesus.
34. I reclaim all the ground I have lost to the enemy in the name of Jesus.
35. Let the blood of Jesus speak against every power working against my marriage.
36. I apply the blood of Jesus to remove all consequences of evil operations and oppression in Jesus' name.
37. I break the binding effect of anything of evil ever put upon me from any source in the name of Jesus.
38. I remove the right of the enemy to afflict my plan to get married in the name of Jesus.
39. I break every bondage of inherited marital confusion in the name of Jesus.
40. I bind and plunder the goods of every strongman plans attached to my marriage plans, in the name of Jesus.
41. Let the angels of the living God roll away the stone blocking my marital breakthroughs, in Jesus' name.
42. Let God arise and let all the enemies of my marital breakthroughs be scattered in the name of Jesus.

43. Let the fire of God melt away the stones hindering my marital blessings in the mighty name of Jesus.
44. Let the cloud blocking the sunlight of my marital breakthrough be dispersed in Jesus' name.
45. Let all evil spirits masquerading to trouble my marital life, be bound in the name of Jesus.
46. Lord, let wonderful changes be my lot this year.
47. Lord, turn away all that would jilt, disappoint or fail me in the name of Jesus.
48. Thank God for the victory.

Prayer Section

Eight

DIVINE FAVOUR

INTRODUCTION
The favour of the Lord will bring a man from grass to grace. It will make a beggar become a prince. For any Christian to make it in life, you need the favour of God. This favour comes when the face of God shines upon a person. It is Gods desire to favour His children. When divine favour is released by God, He will bless you beyond your wildest dreams and people will stumble upon themselves to bestow favour upon you, simply because you are in favour with God.

CONFESSION

Psalm 30:5- *"For His anger is but for a moment, His favour is for life. Weeping may endure the night, but Joy cometh in the morning."*
Psalm31:16- *"Make your face shine upon your servant; save me for your mercies sake."*

PRAISE WORSHIP

PRAYERS

1. Every anti-favour spirit working against my success, die in the name of Jesus.
2. Oil of favour from the throne of God, fall upon my life, in the name of Jesus.
3. Doors of favour, open unto me by fire, in Jesus name.
4. O God arise, make your face to shine upon me, baptise my head with favour, in the name of Jesus.
5. Uncommon favour for divine promotion, come upon my life now, in the name of Jesus.
6. My Father, my Father, my Father, after the order of Esther, give me favour and let me obtain favour in the sight of God and man, in the name of Jesus.
7. I receive the goodness of the Lord in the land of the living, in the name of Jesus.
8. Lord Jesus, deal bountifully with me this year, in the name of Jesus.
9. It does not matter, whether I deserve it or not, I receive unquantifiable favour from the Lord, in the name of Jesus.
10. Oh Lord, as Abraham received favour in your sight, let me receive your favour, so that I can excel in every area of my life.

11. Every blessing God has earmarked for me this year will not pass me by, in the name of Jesus.
12. I shall prevail with man and with God, in the name of Jesus.
13. Oh Lord, let your favour encompass me this year, in the name of Jesus.
14. Let all advice given against my favour, crash and disintegrate in the name of Jesus.
15. I remove my name from the book of failure and backward movement, in the name of Jesus.
16. I claim the power to overcome and to excel among all my contemporaries, in the name of Jesus.
17. Let every negative word and pronouncement made against my success be completely nullified, in the name of Jesus.
18. I receive the anointing for supernatural breakthroughs in the name of Jesus.
19. Every power, drying up the oil of favour on my head, die in the name of Jesus.
20. Father, make it possible for me to find favour in the sight of my helpers, in the name of Jesus.
21. Lord, let me find favour, compassion and loving kindness with all my destiny helpers, in the name of Jesus.
22. Oh Lord bring me into favour with all those who will decide on my advancement, in the name of Jesus.

23. Oh Lord catapult me to greatness, as you did to Daniel in the land of Babylon, in Jesus name.
24. Let the mark of the blood of Jesus, for divine favour and protection, be upon my life, in Jesus name.
25. Oh Lord despatch your angels to roll away every stumbling block to my divine, promotion, advancement and elevation, in the name of Jesus.
26. O Lord let the spirit of favour be upon me everywhere I go, in the name of Jesus.
27. I release the angels of the Lord in the mighty name of Jesus, to go and create favour for all that concerns me.
28. Wherever I have been rejected, let me be accepted in the name of Jesus.
29. Let the spirit of favour and goodwill come upon my life, in the name of Jesus.
30. I reject the spirit of the tail, I claim the spirit of the head, in the name of Jesus.
31. Let favour be upon my life from all directions as from today, in the name of Jesus.
32. Lord Jesus, give unto me this day the key to unlock all doors to my favour and blessings, in the name of Jesus.
33. Divine favour of God, overshadow my life now in the name of Jesus.
34. Lord, let me find favour in your sight, in the name of Jesus.

35. Everything done against me to spoil my favour and joy, receive destruction, in the name of Jesus.

36. O Lord, cause a divine substitution to happen if this is what will move me ahead, in Jesus name.

37. I decree upon my life, that anywhere I go, I will find favour, in the name of Jesus.

38. Let every second, minute, and hour of my life deliver good things unto me, in the name of Jesus.

39. Every evil garment of disfavour, be roasted in Jesus name.

40. Satanic garments of shame and disgrace, I set you ablaze in the name of Jesus.

41. All weapons and devices of the oppressors and tormentors, be rendered impotent, in Jesus name.

42. Holy Ghost, pump favour into my life, in the name of Jesus.

43. Every satanic altar erected against destiny, be destroyed by the fire of the Holy Ghost, in Jesus name.

44. I get the love and favour of all that matter to my destiny and life, in Jesus name.

45. Oh Lord, use my life to advertise your power, in Jesus name.

46. By Your grace Oh Lord, I receive uncommon favour to excel in every area of my life, in Jesus name.

47. Blood of Jesus, disconnect my life from failure at the edge of breakthrough, in the name of Jesus.

48. I refuse to run ahead of God in all my endeavours, in Jesus name.
49. I refuse to act in contrast to Gods will in the name of Jesus.
50. Holy Ghost fire, destroy every satanic magnet attracting disfavour to my life, in the name of Jesus.
51. Oh Lord, plant me by the rivers of prosperity, in Jesus name.
52. Blood of Jesus, speak favour in everything that concerns me from now on, in Jesus name.

Prayer Section

Nine

TEARING OFF THE GARMENT OF SHAME AND DISGRACE

INTRODUCTION

The garment of shame and disgrace is a very terrible thing, and it's one of the wicked materials in the kingdom of darkness. For better understanding, we shall look at the meaning of these components individually.

GARMENT- a garment is a piece of clothing that is sewn to wear on the body for different reasons. Just as some are some for honour and to best fit the occasion they are meant for, even so are some to dishonour.

SHAME- simply means distress or humiliation. To injure the dignity or self respect of a person or one's self.

DISGRACE- simply means dishonour. It is almost similar and closely connected in meaning to shame.

TEAR- To tear means to pull apart or to pull to pieces with some force. It also means to rend apart forcibly. It can also mean to violently twist, wrench or pull off- or apart.

The Bible has a lot to say on this topic-

Who are the ones behind this wickedness? Isaiah 59:5-6 " *They hatch cockatrice eggs, and weave the spider's web; he that eateth of their eggs dieth, and that which is crushed breaketh out into a viper. Their webs shall not become garments, neither shall they cover themselves with their*

works; their works are works of iniquity, and the act of violence is in their hands".

We should note that verse 6 says that their web shall not become garments(plural). This is where it comes from. These powers are majorly witchcraft powers and specialize in making different garments for wicked purposes. One of such garment is the garments of shame and disgrace. There is a department in the covens of darkness which specialize in sewing different garments for their victims. Other causes include sin, iniquity(Isaiah 59:1-2), your foundation (Psalm 11:3), idolatry, powerlessness, curses etc.

Spiritually, a garment is a form of material attached to a force, power or spirit. Isaiah 61:3 *"... the garment of praise for the spirit of heaviness..."*

meaning that a garment can be loaded with spiritual power. Effects of being clothed with the garment of shame and disgrace.

- Setback
- Failure
- Inability to move forward
- Sorrow
- Distress
- Loneliness
- Famine of favour
- Bad luck
- Scarcity of helpers
- Promise and fail syndrome
- Inferiority complex
- Finding it difficult to make a headway in life.

CONFESSION: Psalm 31:17: *'Let me not be ashamed, O LORD; for I have called upon thee: let the wicked be ashamed, and let them be silent in the grave.'*
Psalm 25:2 *'O my God, I trust in thee: let me not be ashamed, let not mine enemies triumph over me.'*

PRAISE WORSHIP

PRAYERS

1. Thank the Lord for His power to deliver from any form of bondage.
2. Holy Spirit energize me to pray to the point of breakthroughs, in the name of Jesus.
3. Pray with this song: *there is power mighty in the blood (2x), there is power mighty in the blood of Jesus Christ, there is power mighty in the blood.*
4. Every mystery of shame and disgrace, upon my life, die by fire, in the name of Jesus.
5. Every garment of shame and disgrace ordained for me by any evil power in my foundation, die, in Jesus name.
6. Every ordination of shame and disgrace done against my destiny on the mat through pressing of sand, programmed into the sun, moon and star, scatter by fire in Jesus name.

7. Garment of shame and disgrace upon my body, catch fire, in the name of Jesus.
8. I tear into pieces every garment of shame and disgrace, in the name of Jesus.
9. Spirit of shame and disgrace, die by fire, in the name of Jesus.
10. Garment of shame and disgrace designed to put me to shame at the place of breakthrough and prosperity, catch fire, in the name of Jesus.
11. Every power weaving the garment of shame for my life, die a shameful death and be silent in the grave, in Jesus name.
12. Every garment of shame and disgrace sown for me by ancestral powers, catch fire in Jesus name.
13. Every garment of shame and disgrace of my father's house that I am wearing, catch fire, in the name of Jesus.
14. Every garment of shame and disgrace of my mother's house that I am wearing, catch fire, in the name of Jesus
15. Every satanic consultation of the children of the bond woman to wear garment of shame for me scatter in Jesus.
16. Throughout the days of my life, I shall not be put to shame in the name of Jesus.
17. Holy Ghost fire, destroy every satanic garment in my life, in the name of Jesus.
18. I reject every garment of shame, in the name of Jesus.

19. I reject every shoe of shame, in the name of Jesus.
20. I reject every headgear and cap of shame, in the name of Jesus.
21. Shamefulness shall not be my lot, in the name of Jesus.
22. I refuse to wear the garment of tribulation and sorrow, in the name of Jesus.
23. Every demonic limitation of my progress as a result of shame, be removed, in the name of Jesus.
24. Every network of shame around me, be paralyzed, in the name of Jesus.
25. Those who seek for my shame shall die for my sake, in the name of Jesus.
26. As far as shame is concerned, I shall not record any point for satan, in the name of Jesus.
27. In the name of Jesus I shall not eat the bread of sorrow, I shall not eat the bread of shame and I shall not eat the bread of defeat.
28. Let every house of shame constructed against me be demolished, in the name of Jesus.
29. Every spirit of shame set in motion against my life; I bind you in the name of Jesus name.
30. I command every agent of spiritual rags to lose its hold over my life, in the name of Jesus.
31. Every garment of hindrance and dirtiness, be dissolved by the fire of the Holy Ghost in the name of Jesus.

32. All those laughing me to scorn shall witness my testimony, in the name of Jesus.
33. Let all the destructive plan of the enemies aimed against me blow up in their faces, in the name of Jesus.
34. I command every garment of infirmity to catch fire in the name of Jesus.
35. I command every garment of satanic delay, to be roasted by fire, in the name of Jesus.
36. I command every garment of demotion to lose its hold over my life, in the name of Jesus.
37. I command every garment of confusion to lose its hold over my life, in the name of Jesus.
38. I command every garment of backward movement to lose its hold over my life, in the name of Jesus.
39. Let my point of ridicule be converted to a source of miracle, in the name of Jesus.
40. Let all powers sponsoring evil decisions against me be disgraced, in the name of Jesus.
41. Let the road be closed against every unprofitable visitation in my life, in the name of Jesus.
42. Garment of glory, favour and honour come upon me, in Jesus name.
43. Lord let wonderful changes be my lot this year, in the name of Jesus.
44. I command all human woes to find me untouchable, in Jesus name.

45. I remove my name from the book of failure and moving backward, in the name of Jesus.
46. I paralyse the handiwork of household wickedness and envious agents in all matters concerning me, in the name of Jesus.
47. Holy Ghost seal all pockets that have demonic holes, in the name of Jesus.
48. Let every evil trend directing my affairs be reversed, in the name of Jesus.
49. Let every architect of problems receive termination, in the name of Jesus.
50. I refuse to reap in any satanic harvest for my life, in the name of Jesus.
51. I paralyse all spiritual wolves working against my life, in the name of Jesus.
53. That which hinders greatness, begin to give way now, in the name of Jesus.
54. Any negative transaction currently affecting my life negatively, be cancelled, in the name of Jesus.
55. I command all the dark works done against me in secret to be exposed and nullified in the name of Jesus.
56. Let the blood in the Cross stand between me and any dark work done against me.

57. Let the power of the blood of Jesus be released on my behalf and let it speak against every stubborn situation in my life.
58. O Lord let the mischief of the oppressors come upon their own heads in the name of Jesus.
59. I defeat, paralyse and erase . . . . (Pick from the under listed) by the blood of Jesus.
- Spirit of demotion
- Failure at the edge of miracles
- Vision killers
- Marital problems
- Financial downgrading
- Inherited problems
- Dream attackers
60. I frustrate and disappoint every instrument of the enemy fashioned against me, in the name of Jesus.
61. Let the displacing power of the Holy Spirit displace any darkness in my life and replace it with light.
62. O Lord give me the power to embarrass my enemies.
63. Father, bring help from above and disgrace my oppressors.
64. Every curse, issued against me, enforcing shame and disgrace in my life, die, in the name of Jesus.
65. When you mention any of the under-listed curses, you will aggressively say, "break, break, break, in the name of Jesus. I release myself from you in the name of Jesus".

- Every curse of failure and defeat
- Every curse of poverty
- Every curse of oppression
- Every curse of bad reputation
- Every curse of personal destruction or suicide
- Every curse of profitless hard work
- Every curse of mental and physical sickness
- Every curse of evil dedication
- Every curse of family strife
- Every curse of the reproductive organ
- Every curse of witchcraft
- Every curse of sickness and infirmity

66. O Lord, convert every failure in my life to success.
67. O Lord, convert every frustration in my life to fulfilment.
68. O Lord, convert every rejection in my life to acceptance.
69. O Lord, convert every pain in my life to pleasure.
70. O Lord, convert every poverty in my life to blessing.
71. O Lord, convert every mistake in my life to perfection.
72. O Lord, convert every sickness in my life to health.
73. This very day, in the name of Jesus, I shall . . .

- Receive my deliverance
- Receive my breakthroughs
- Receive joy, instead of sorrow and shame

- Receive the touch of God
- Receive the touch of God
- Receive divine solution to my life's problem
- Laugh last. My enemies shall cry.
74. I reject the spirit of regret, woes and disappointment, in the name of Jesus.
75. I reject the spirit of impossibility; I claim open doors, in the name of Jesus.
76. Lord, make my case a miracle. Shock my foes, friends, and even myself, in the name of Jesus.
77. Blood of Jesus remove any un-progressive label from every aspect of my life.
78. Let the spiritual rag of poverty in my life be destroyed by the fire of God, in the name of Jesus.
79. Let every enemy of excellence in my life be paralysed, in Jesus name.
80. Let the shame of my enemies be greatly multiplied.
81. O Lord, let the defeat and disgrace of the enemies of my progress be nullified beyond measure.
82. Every lame glory, receive life now, in the name of Jesus.
83. Lord, give me the power for a new beginning.
84. Lord Jesus, I thank you for answering my prayer.

Prayer Section

Ten

DIVINE REVELATION

INTRODUCTION
Unto every man created by God, there are divine secrets that will make an individual unique and prosper in life. Revelation of who you are or what God made you to be and the steps to becoming it, is a summary of your divine purpose on earth.

WHY MUST WE KNOW WHO WE ARE?
1. To find our place in life.
2. To know how to better serve, glorify, worship and obey God.
3. To know our destiny, our divine purpose on Earth.
4. It enables us to know our talents, potentials and virtues.
5. Prepares us and gives us understanding of our uniqueness, ability, capability. It also gives us a clear insight on the kind of partner we will need for the fulfillment of your destiny.

THE BENEFITS OF DIVINE REVELATION.
1. Ways will be open to you.
2. Where others find it difficult to survive, prosper and excel, you will find it easy to do so.
3. You will have peace of mind.
4. Blessing, favour, grace and untold wealth will be at your reach.
5. You will be strong and victorious, because you are well informed.

SCRIPTURE READING: Job 29:4, Psalm 25:14, Daniel 2:22, Job 12:22, Duet 29:29, Dan 2:22, Psalm 25:14, Eph 1:17

Confessions - Psalm 20:7-8 *'Some trust in chariots, and some in horses: but we will remember the name of the LORD our God. They are brought down and fallen: but we are risen, and stand upright.'*
Deut 29:29: *The secret things belong unto the LORD our God: but those things which are revealed belong unto us and to our children for ever, that we may do all the words of this law.*
Ps 5:8: *Lead me, O LORD, in thy righteousness because of mine enemies; make thy way straight before my face.*
Ps 25:14: *The secret of the LORD is with them that fear him; and he will shew them his covenant.*
Dan 2:22: *He revealeth the deep and secret things: he knoweth what is in the darkness, and the light dwelleth with him.*
Eph 1:17: *That the God of our Lord Jesus Christ, the Father of glory, may give unto you the spirit of wisdom and revelation in the knowledge of him.*

PRAISE WORSHIP

PRAYER POINTS

1. Thank God for the revelation power of the Holy Spirit.
2. My heavens, open by fire in the name of Jesus.
3. In this programme, O Lord I divorce my own will to receive God's will, in Jesus name.
4. Father, deliver me from the bondage of sin and spiritual laziness.
5. O Lord, forgive me for every fake motive or thought that has ever formed in my heart since the day I was born.
6. O Lord, forgive me for every lie that I have ever told against any person, system or organization.
7. O Lord, remove from me, any persistent buried grudges, half-acknowledged enmity against anyone and every other thing that can block my spiritual vision, in the name of Jesus.
8. Father Lord, inject into me your spiritual vitamins that will produce hunger and thirst for prayers in me, in the name of Jesus
9. Let Christ dwell in my heart by faith in Jesus name.
10. Let utterance be given unto me to make known the mystery of the Gospel, in the name of Jesus.

11. Father, open my spiritual understanding.
12. Father, I lose myself in You.
13. O Lord, give unto me the spirit of revelation and wisdom in the knowledge of You.
14. I anoint my eyes and ears with the blood of Jesus, that they may see and hear wondrous things from heaven.
15. I receive the unsearchable wisdom in the Holy Ghost, in the name of Jesus.
16. Father Lord, guide me and direct me in knowing Your mind concerning my life.
17. Anything in me working against the power of God, die by fire, in Jesus name.
18. Every spiritual leakage, close, in the name of Jesus.
19. I challenge every organ of my body with the fire of the Holy Spirit. (*Lay your right hand on various parts of your body, beginning from the head*), in the name of Jesus.
20. Every mystery of darkness, scatter in the name of Jesus.
21. O Lord, remove spiritual cataract from my eyes.
22. Any power blocking the vision of God for my life, your time is up, die, in Jesus name.
23. Vision of the Almighty God, my life is available, enter in Jesus name.
24. Powers of my father's house, blocking my vision, die, in the name of Jesus.

25. Every evil veil covering my eyes, catch fire in Jesus name.
26. Secrets of my life, come upon my tabernacle, in Jesus name.
27. O Lord, teach me deep and secret things.
28. Father, open my eyes to all I should see on this issue.
29. O Lord, give me divine wisdom to operate my life.
30. Holy Spirit, uncover my darkest secrets, in the name of Jesus.
31. Heavenly Father, reveal myself to me.
32. O God, to whom no secret is hidden, make known unto me the secret of my life.
33. O God my Father, show me the blueprint for my life.
34. Lord, make Your way plain unto me.
35. Father, reveal to me secrets that will move my life forward, in the name of Jesus.
36. Holy Spirit, open my eyes to see beyond the visible and make the invisible real to me, in the name of Jesus.
37. Let every dirtiness blocking my communication pipe with the living God be washed clean with the blood of Jesus, in the name of Jesus.
38. Let the Spirit of prophecy and revelation fall upon the totality of my being, in the name of Jesus.
39. O Lord, make me a vessel capable of knowing your secret things.

40. I refuse to fall under the manipulation of the spirit of confusion.
41. I stand against any satanic attachments that may seek to confuse and manipulate any revelation I receive about myself, from You in Jesus name.
42. Let every power planning to turn my life upside-down, fall down and die now, in the name of Jesus.
43. I paralyse every satanic inspiration targeted against me, in the name of Jesus.
44. I barricade my life from satanic opinions, in the name of Jesus.
45. Let my divinely-appointed helpers begin to locate me from now, in the name of Jesus.
46. Power of divine beneficial secrets, come upon my life, in Jesus name.
47. O Lord, teach me to know that which is worth knowing and love that which is worth loving, and to dislike whatsoever is not pleasing unto You.
48. Heavenly Father, expose the activities of unfriendly friends in my life.
49. I bind the activities of . . . (pick from the list below) in my life, in the name of Jesus.

- Demonic manipulation in dreams and visions
- Confusing revelations
- Spiritual blindness and deafness
- Unprofitable advice
- Ungodly impatience

50. If I . . . (mention your name) have missed my way, O Lord re-direct my steps in Jesus name.
51. O Lord, defend your interest in my life.
53. Let the eagle in my life come alive and fly, in the name of Jesus.
54. O Lord, let me be wholly available to You on this earth, in the name of Jesus.
55. I shall not live for nothing, in the name of Jesus.
56. All my chained blessings be unchained, in the name of Jesus.
57. All spiritual cages, inhibiting my progress, roast by the fire of the Holy Spirit, in the name of Jesus.
58. O Lord, reveal to me every secret behind any problem I have.
59. All Lord let me know all I should know about this issue (*mention the issue*)
60. I receive power to operate with sharp spiritual eyes that cannot be deceived, in the name of Jesus.
61. Glory and power of the Almighty God, fall upon me in a mighty way, in the name of Jesus.
62. I remove my name from the book of those who grope

63. Divine revelations, spiritual visions, dreams and information will not become a scarce commodity in my life, in the name of Jesus.
64. I drink to the full from the well of salvation and anointing, in the name of Jesus.
65. Every idol present in my heart consciously or unconsciously concerning this issue, melt away by the fire of the Holy Spirit, in the name of Jesus.
66. I refuse to make foundational mistakes in my decision making in the name of Jesus.
67. Holy Spirit open my eyes and help me to take the right decision, in the name of Jesus.
68. Thank you Jesus for you presence and good testimonies.
69. If you have received the gift of speaking in tongues, pray in the spirit for at least 15minutes before going to bed.

Prayer Section

Eleven

BREAKING EVERY EVIL DEDICATION

INTRODUCTION

It is your responsibility to appropriate the curse breaking power of Christ to get rid of any effect of dedication to the power of darkness.

Numbers 6:27: *"And they shall put my name upon the children of Israel; and I will bless them"*.

God can only bless those that have been dedicated to Him. He can only bless those that have His name upon their lives. There are many people that God cannot bless because of their evil dedication; those dedicated to evil spirits, family idols, family shrines, river spirits etc. Jabez cried out to God, *"O that thou would bless me indeed, and enlarge my coast, and that thy hand might be with me and thou would keep me from evil that it will not grieve me! And the Lord granted his request"* (1 Chronicles 4:10). His name which means "born in sorrow' glorified the devil. When Jabez cried out, God heard him and granted his request. The Bible records that he was more honourable than his brethren.

Have you been dedicated to an idol, to a shrine or evil spirit unknowingly or knowingly? Does your name glorify God? As you cry out to Him in prayers, He will revoke every evil dedication in your life, in the name of Jesus.

CONFESSIONS

Isaiah 52:3 *"For thus saith the Lord, 'You have sold yourselves for nothing, And you shall be redeemed without money'"*.

PRAISE WORSHIP

PRAYER POINTS

1. Thank the Lord for His power to deliver from any form of bondage.
2. Thank the Lord for the redeeming power in the blood of Jesus.
3. I confess the sins of my ancestors (list them).
4. Ask the Lord for forgiveness.
5. Ask the Lord to forgive those sins you do not know about.
6. Holy Ghost incubate me with Your fire, in the name of Jesus.
7. Mystery of evil dedication over my life, die in the name of Jesus.
8. Let the power in the blood of Jesus separate me from the sins of my ancestors, in the name of Jesus.
9. O Lord, send your axe of fire to the foundation of my life and destroy every evil plantation there.

10. I reject any stamp or seal, placed upon me by ancestral spirits, in the name of Jesus.

11. I release myself from every inherited bondage, in Jesus name.

12. I release myself from every evil domination and control, in the name of Jesus.

13. I renounce every evil dedication placed upon my life, in Jesus name.

14. I break any evil edict and ordination, in the name of Jesus.

15. The rod of the wicked rising against my family line, be rendered impotent for my sake in the name of Jesus.

16. I release myself from the grip of any idol I have been dedicated to as a child, in the name of Jesus.

17. I release myself from every negative anointing, in the name of Jesus.

18. Pray in the Spirit, if you have received the baptism of the Holy Spirit, for 15mins.

19. All evil marks on my body, burn off by the fire of the Holy Ghost, in the name of Jesus.

20. Every door of spiritual leakage, close, in the name of Jesus.

21. I release myself from every spiritual pollution emanating from my parents religion, in the name of Jesus.

22. I lose myself from any dark spirit, in the name of Jesus.

23. Every negative transaction done against my life while I was in my mother's womb, currently affecting my life, be

24. Let the gate opened to the enemy by my foundation be closed forever with the blood of Jesus.
25. Every problem attached to my name be revoked, in the name of Jesus.
26. Blood of Jesus nullify every evil consequences of any blood that was shed on my naming ceremony.
27. Blood of Jesus, release my life from the grip of any problem transferred into my life from the womb, in the name of Jesus.
28. You idol of my father's house loose me and let me go, in the name of Jesus.
29. You idol of my mother's house loose me and let me go, in the name of Jesus
30. I renounce and loose myself from every negative dedication placed upon my life, in the name of Jesus.
31. I command all demons associated with the dedication to leave now, in the name of Jesus.
32. Every satanic altar in my father's house bearing my name and picture on it, be destroyed by the fire of the Holy Ghost in the name of Jesus.
33. Every satanic animal that I have been dedicated to as a child, be separated from me by fire in the name of Jesus.
34. Song "God of deliverance, send down fire....." (sing for about 15 minutes, clapping your hands)

35. I take authority over all associated curses, in the name of Jesus.

36. Lord, cancel the evil consequences of any broken demonic promise or dedication, in the name of Jesus.

37. I take authority over all the curses emanating from broken dedication, in the name of Jesus.

38. I command all demons associated with any broken evil parental vow and dedication to depart from me now, in Jesus' name.

39. I break and loose myself from every evil inherited curse and covenant, in the name of Jesus.

40. Ask the Lord to remove the curse if it is from Him.

41. I vomit every evil food that I have been fed with as a child, in the name of Jesus.

42. Satanic food given to me on my naming ceremony......... (kolanut, alligator pepper, *mention them*), I vomit you by fire in the name of Jesus.

43. Finger of God, enter into my stomach now, and push out every satanic food that I have eaten as a child, in the name of Jesus.

44. Every sacrifice, done on my behalf, for one form of atonement or the other, be nullified now by the blood of Jesus, in the name of Jesus.

45. Every foundational poison, circulating around my body, be arrested in the name of Jesus.
46. Hand of the living God, remove my life and destiny out of every cage of darkness, in the name of Jesus.
47. I cancel all the consequences of any evil local name attached to my person, in the name of Jesus.
48. Oh Lord give me a new inner man, if I have been altered, in the name of Jesus.
49. Oh Lord, if I have fallen behind in any area of my life as a result of satanic dedication, empower me to recover all lost opportunities and wasted years, in the name of Jesus.
50. Any power, that wants to draw me away from the presence of the Lord, to destroy me, die in the name of Jesus.
51. Any power, that wants me to fulfil my destiny partially, die in the name of Jesus.
52. All satanic manipulations, aimed at changing my destiny, be frustrated, in the name of Jesus.
53. I command all foundational strongmen attached to my life to be paralysed, in the name of Jesus.
54. Every evil effect of any strange touch, be removed from my life, in the name of Jesus.
55. Arrows of deliverance, locate my destiny, in the name of Jesus.
56. I dis-sociate my life from every name given to me under satanic anointing, in Jesus name.

57. Let any record of my names in the demonic world be wiped off by the blood of Jesus.

58. I break and smash to pieces every curse and evil covenant attached to my names, in the name of Jesus.

59. I break the flow of any evil river coming into my life through unprofitable names, in the name of Jesus.

60. I cancel the influence of family idols attached to my name, in Jesus name.

61. Every familiar and wicked spirit behind my names, get out of my life, in Jesus name.

62. Every witchcraft naming, be dissolved from my fore-head and navel, in Jesus name.

63. My new name.........(mention it), bind me to the blood of Jesus and to prosperity, in the name of Jesus.

64. Every hidden or silent name given to me to destroy my life on my naming ceremony day, I nullify you in Jesus name.

65. Holy Spirit, take control of any negative situation my names have caused me, in Jesus name.

66. You evil foundational plantations, come out of my life with all your roots, in the name of Jesus.

67. Lord Jesus walk back into every second of my life and deliver me where I need deliverance, heal me where I need healing, transform me where I need transformation, in Jesus name.

68. I release myself from every ancestral demonic pollution, in the name of Jesus.
69. I cut myself off from every spirit of....... (mention the name of your place of birth), in the name of Jesus.
70. I cut myself off from every tribal spirit and curse, in Jesus name.
71. I cut myself off from every territorial spirit and curse, in the name of Jesus.
72. I disconnect myself from any conscious or unconscious linkage with demonic spirits, in the name of Jesus.
73. Holy Ghost fire purge my life, in the name of Jesus.
74. I release myself from the cage of family captivity, in the name of Jesus.
75. Every effect of evil dedication upon my life, come out with all your roots in Jesus name.
76. Let my name be erased from every satanic records of my family line, in the name of Jesus.
77. I break all covenants inherited from my mother's and father's lineage, in the name of Jesus.
78. I hereby confess total separation from any evil dedication, in the name of Jesus.
79. I move from bondage to liberty, in the name of Jesus.
80. I receive the seal of the Holy Spirit upon my life, in the name of Jesus.
81. I rededicate my life back to the Lord Jesus Christ, in the name of Jesus.
82. Make each of the following powerful confessions 7 times

* Through the blood of Jesus, I have been redeemed out of the hands of the devil.
* I walk in the light and the blood of Jesus cleanses me from all sins.
* Through the blood of Jesus I am justified, sanctified and made holy with Gods holiness
* Through the blood of Jesus, I have the life of God in me.
* Through the blood of Jesus, I have access to the presence of the Lord.

Prayer Section

Twelve

GAINING FREEDOM FROM SPIRIT SPOUSE

INTRODUCTION

The problem of spirit husband and spirit wife is one of the greatest problems which has pervaded all societies of the world. Contrary to popular perception, it is not a problem that is restricted to the African environment, but also the entire human race is involved. Though it has been grossly neglected for too long but this does not rule out the fact that it is real still very active in human lives today. Some who have had problems in this area have decided to keep mute since disclosing their strange experiences is capable of making others view them as strange fellows. Many have even grappled with bizarre dream experiences that cannot be shared with other people and they have remained under bondage, as no one seems to be able to provide solution to their problems.

Incase the subject still sounds strange to you, beloved, there are a lot of activities in people's lives sponsored by the spirit spouse as evidences to look out for whenever they are in operation. These evil spirits are so jealous and heartless that they oversee such activities as destruction of virtues, late marriages, misfortune, profitless hard-work, marital confusion among many others. But the fact you should absorb now beloved is that you can overcome their powers and activities. The prayer points given below will serve as guidelines to addressing them and breaking loose from their grip forever, in the name of Jesus.

110

CONFESSION: ROMANS 16:20 *'And the God of peace shall bruise Satan under your feet shortly. The grace of our Lord Jesus Christ be with you. Amen.'*

PRAISE WORSHIP

PRAYER POINTS

1. Spirit husband/wife, release me by fire, in the name of Jesus.
2. Every spirit husband/wife, I divorce you by the blood of Jesus, in the name of Jesus.
3. Every spirit wife/husband, die, in the name of Jesus.
4. Everything you have deposited in my life, come out by fire, in the name of Jesus.
5. Every power that is working against my marriage, fall down and die, in the name of Jesus.
6. I divorce and renounce my marriage with the spirit husband/wife, in the name of Jesus.
7. I break all covenants entered into with the spirit husband/wife, in the name of Jesus.
8. I command the thunder fire of God to burn into ashes the wedding gown, ring, photographs, and all other materials used for the marriage, in the name of Jesus.
9. I send the fire of God to burn to ashes the marriage certificate, in the name of Jesus.

10. I break every blood and soul-tie covenant with the spirit husband/wife, in the name of Jesus.
11. I send the thunder fire of God to burn to ashes the children born into the marriage, in the name of Jesus.
12. I withdraw my blood, sperm/egg, or any other part of my body deposited on the altar of the spirit husband/wife, in the name of Jesus.
13. You spirit husband/wife, tormenting my life and earthly marriage, I bind you with hot chains and fetters of God and cast you out of my life into the deep pit and I command you not to ever come into my life again, in the name of Jesus.
14. I return to you every property of yours in my possession in the spirit world including the dowry and whatsoever was used for the marriage and covenant, in the name of Jesus.
15. I drain myself of all evil materials deposited in my body as a result of our sexual relation, in the name of Jesus.
16. Lord, send Holy Ghost fire into my root and burn out all unclean things deposited in it by the spirit husband/wife, in the name of Jesus.
17. I break the head of the snake deposited into my body by the spirit husband/wife to do me harm and command it to come out, in the name of Jesus.
18. I purge out with the blood of Jesus, every evil material deposited in my body to prevent my from having children on earth, in the name of Jesus.

19. Lord repair and restore every damage done to any part of my body and my earthly marriage by the spirit husband/wife, in the name of Jesus.
20. I reject and cancel, every curse, evil pronouncement, jinx, spell, enchantment and incantation placed upon me by the spirit husband or wife, in the name of Jesus.
21. I command the spirit husband/wife to turn his/her back on me forever, in the name of Jesus.
22. I renounce and reject the name given to me by the spirit husband/wife, in the name of Jesus.
23. I hereby declare and confess that the Lord Jesus Christ is my spouse for eternity, in the name of Jesus.
24. I sock myself in the blood of Jesus and cancel the evil mark or writings placed on me, in the name of Jesus.
25. I set myself free from the stronghold and domineering power and bondage of the spirit husband/wife, in the name of Jesus.
26. I paralyse the remote control power and work used to destabilize my earthly marriage and to prevent me from bearing children in my earthly marriage, in the name of Jesus.
27. I announce to the heavens that I am married forever to Jesus, in the name of Jesus.
28. Every trademark of evil, be shaken out of my life, in the name of Jesus.

29. Every evil writing engraved by iron pen, be wiped off by the blood of Jesus, in the name of Jesus.

30. I bring the blood of Jesus upon the spirit that does not want to go, in the name of Jesus.

31. I bring the blood of Jesus on every evidence that can be tendered by wicked spirits against me, in the name of Jesus.

32. I file a counter report in the heavens against every evil marriage, in the name of Jesus.

33. I refuse to supply any evidence that the enemy may use against me, in the name of Jesus.

34. Let satanic exhibition be destroyed by the blood of Jesus, in the name of Jesus.

35. I declare to you spirit husband/wife that there is no vacancy for you in my life, in the name of Jesus.

36. O Lord make me a vehicle of deliverance, in the name of Jesus.

37. I com by faith to Mount Zion. Lord command deliverance upon my life now, in the name of Jesus.

38. Lord water me from the waters of God, in the name of Jesus.

39. I take back and possess all my earthly belongings, in the custody of the spirit husband/wife, in the name of Jesus.

40. Let the careful siege of the enemy be dismantled, in the name of Jesus.

41. O Lord, defend your interest in my life, in the name of Jesus.

42. Everything written in the cycle of the moon against me, be blotted out, in the name of Jesus.

43. Everything programmed into the sun, moon and stars against me, be dismantled, in the name of Jesus.

44. Every evil thing programmed into my genes, be blotted out, by the blood of Jesus, in the name of Jesus.

45. O Lord shake out seasons of failure and frustration from my life, in the name of Jesus.

46. I overthrow every wicked law working against my life, in the name of Jesus.

47. I ordain a new time, season, and profitable law, in the name of Jesus.

48. I speak destruction unto the palaces of the queens of the coasts and of the rivers, in the name of Jesus.

49. I speak destruction unto the headquarters of the spirit of Egypt and blow up their altars, in the name of Jesus.

50. I speak destructions unto the altars speaking against the purpose of God for my life, in the name of Jesus.

51. I declare myself a virgin for the Lord, in the name of Jesus.

52. Let every evil veil upon my life be torn open, in the name of Jesus.

53. Every wall between me and the visitation of God, be broken, in the name of Jesus.

54. Let the counsel of God prosper in my life, in the name of Jesus.

55. I destroy the power of any demonic seed in my life from the womb, in the name of Jesus.

56. I speak unto my umbilical gate to overthrow all negative parental spirits, in the name of Jesus.

57. I break the yoke of the spirit having access to my reproductive gate, in the name of Jesus.

58. O Lord, let your time of refreshing come upon me, in the name of Jesus.

59. I bring fire from the altar of the Lord upon every evil marriage, in the name of Jesus.

60. I redeem myself by the blood of Jesus from every sex trap, in the name of Jesus.

61. I erase the engraving of my name on any evil marriage record, in the name of Jesus.

62. I reject and renounce every evil spiritual marriage, in the name of Jesus.

63. I confess that Jesus is my original spouse and He is jealous over me, in the name of Jesus.

64. I issue a bill of divorcement to every spirit wife/husband, in the name of Jesus.

65. I bind every spirit wife/husband with everlasting chains, in the name of Jesus.

66. Let heavenly testimony overcome every evil testimony of hell over my life, in the name of Jesus.
67. O Lord bring to my remembrance every spiritual trap and contract, in the name of Jesus.
68. Let the blood of Jesus purge me of every contaminating material, in the name of Jesus.
69. Let the spirit husband or wife, fall down and die, in the name of Jesus.
70. Let all your children attached to me fall down and die, in the name of Jesus.
71. I burn your certificate and destroy your ring, in the name of Jesus.
72. I execute judgment against water spirit and I declare that you are reserved for everlasting chains in darkness, in the name of Jesus.
73. O Lord contend with those that are contending with me, in the name of Jesus.
74. Every trademark of water spirits, be shaken out of my life, in the name of Jesus.

Prayer Section

Thirteen

BREAKING THE BACKBONE OF POVERTY AND GAINING FINANCIAL DOMINION

INTRODUCTION

Poverty is a horrible spirit. It has ruined many lives, destroyed many marriages as well as numerous destinies. The spirit of poverty is responsible for:

- Pockets that leak; when you find out that your money goes mysteriously.
- When you find out that all attempts to make money ends up in failure.
- When you are consistently being defrauded either in business or in mysterious encounters.
- When you consistently find out that what should be a profitable opportunity ends up landing you in debt.
- When you are always the victim of armed robbers, thieves and financial criminals.
- When you find out that all your employees are '*rat*' workers- they steal your money, raw materials and products, they don't do their work and are always destroying company property and equipment.
- When you cannot make headway in your profession, job or business despite your skills, connections and innovative ideas.

If you find any of the above patterns repeating itself or any of the characteristics manifesting itself in your life, it is an indication that you need to be delivered from the spirit of poverty. If you are poor, it will be extremely difficult for you to get married as you will be unable to pay for the basic necessities that you will need as a married man/woman e.g. accommodation, feeding, clothing etc. The following prayer points will destroy the backbone of the spirit of poverty in your life and will usher you into dumbfounding financial breakthroughs. As you pray them, you will definitely share your own testimony in the mighty name of Jesus!!

CONFESSION:

2 COR. 8:9 "For you know the grace of our Lord Jesus Christ that though he was rich, yet for my sake he became poor, so that I through his poverty may become rich."
DEUT. 8:18 "But remember the Lord your God for it is he who gives me the ability to make wealth, and so confirms his covenant, which he swore to my forefathers as it is today."
3 JOHN 2 "Dearly beloved, I wish above all things that thou mayest be in good health and prosper, even as thy soul prospereth."

PRAISE WORSHIP
PRAYER POINTS

1. O God, arise and let my head be lifted up, in the name of Jesus.
2. Every witchcraft-sponsored poverty, die, in the name of Jesus.
3. Every altar in my place of birth working against my prosperity, burn to ashes, in the name of Jesus.
4. Every satanic priest ministering against my prosperity on any evil altar, die by fire, in the name of Jesus.
5. Every strength and power of any environmental altar wishing against my life, wither in the name of Jesus.
6. Today, I raise the altar of continuous prosperity upon my destiny, in the name of Jesus.
7. Every stronghold of physical and spiritual poverty in my life, be pulled down by fire in the name of Jesus.
8. Any covenant in my life that is strengthening the stronghold of poverty, break, in the name of Jesus.
9. Every stronghold of poverty where I am living now and in my place of work, I pull you down, in the name of Jesus.
10. O Lord, create opportunities for my prosperity today in the name of Jesus.
11. I bind and cast out every negative word enforcing poverty upon my life in the name of Jesus.
12. Spirit of stinginess, disappear from my life in the name of Jesus.

13. I bind and cast out the spirit of disobedience in the name of Jesus.
14. Where other people are spending money, I refuse to spend boldface in the name of Jesus.
15. Every evil machinery against my prosperity, be destroyed in the name of Jesus.
16. I destroy by fire, every weapon of poverty targeted against my life in the name o Jesus.
17. Every descendant of poverty in my life, fall down and die, in the name of Jesus.
18. Every evil power sitting on my prosperity, somersault and die, in the name of Jesus.
19. I break every caldron of poverty in my life, in the name of Jesus.
20. You stronghold of poverty, receive the fire of God, in the name of Jesus.
21. I cut myself and my family off, from every inherited poverty, in the name of Jesus.
22. Every stigma of poverty in my life, be rubbed off by the blood of Jesus, in the name of Jesus.
23. Every adjustment to humiliate me, I rebel against you, in the name of Jesus.
24. Every power adjusting my life to poverty, fall down and die, in the name of Jesus.
25. I shall not adjust to poverty, in the name of Jesus.
26. Holy Spirit, adjust my life to prosperity, in the name of Jesus.

27. You network chains of failure rattling my life, melt by fire in the name of Jesus.

28. You anchor of failure holding my destiny, break, in the name of Jesus.

29. Every spiritual chain of slavery upon my life, break by fire, in the name of Jesus.

30. Every chain of inherited failure upon my life, break by fire, in the name of Jesus.

31. Let every evil seed of generational poverty, dry up, in the name of Jesus.

32. I command the stronghold of inherited poverty in my life to be pulled down, by the blood of Jesus, in the name of Jesus.

33. Holy Ghost, arrest on my behalf every spirit of poverty in the name of Jesus.

34. I dismantle every demonic opposition to my prosperity, in the name of Jesus.

35. Every satanic river of poverty and failure, dry up by fire, in the name of Jesus.

36. Every altar of poverty prepared by my ancestors, break now, in the name of Jesus.

37. Every witchcraft assembly in my neighborhood, be scattered by Holy Ghost fire, in the name of Jesus.

38. Let the stubborn strongman of poverty in my place of birth (*mention the place*) be paralyzed by fire, in the name of Jesus.

39. Every territorial spirit working against my prosperity be chained in the name of Jesus.
40. Every covenant made at my birth and in my place of birth, break in the name of Jesus.
41. Every witchcraft covenant of poverty affecting my prosperity, break in the name of Jesus.
42. Every covenant of poverty made by the living or the dead against my prosperity, break in the name of Jesus.
43. Hear, O heavens, I am dead to the covenant of poverty; I am alive to the covenant of prosperity in the name of Jesus.
44. Every arrow of poverty, fired into my life, come out with all your roots, in the name of Jesus.
45. Every curse of poverty, placed upon my family, be consumed by fire, in the name of Jesus.
46. Every curse of poverty fired into my life by household wickedness, go back to your sender, in the name of Jesus.
47. As a result of my prosperity prayers, I receive the mandate to enter into the covenant of wealth, in the name of Jesus.
48. O Lord, empower me to pluck the seed of wealth that will swallow poverty in my life, in the name of Jesus.
49. From today, my portion has changed from that of a beggar and borrower to that of a lender and giver, in the name of Jesus.
50. Every sponsored dream of poverty by household wickedness against my life, vanish in the name of Jesus.

51. Every satanic banker representing me in the spirit world, fall down and die, in the name of Jesus.
52. Every evil bank established against my destiny, be liquidated by fire, in the name of Jesus,
53. Every Egyptian poverty, I shall see you no more, in the name of Jesus.
54. I command the thunder of God to break into pieces, all the satanic arrows of poverty fired into my life, in the name of Jesus.
55. Every foundational arrow of poverty, be removed by fire in the name of Jesus.
56. I paralyze all the inherited arrows of poverty in the name of Jesus.
57. Father Lord, shield me against any arrow of poverty in the name of Jesus.
58. Every cage of poverty, roast to ashes in the name of Jesus.
59. Every satanic barrier designed to hold me back from my desired position, be shattered to pieces in the name of Jesus.
60. Every instrument of failure, working against my advancement, I command you to fail, in the name of Jesus.
61. Let every evil decree working against my potentials be revoked in the name of Jesus.
62. I remove by fire every mark of poverty upon my life, in the name of Jesus.

63. My life, my business, reject all marks of poverty in the name of Jesus.

64. Every evil hand that carried me when I was a baby, roast by fire in the name of Jesus.

65. You mountain of debt, programmed to put me into poverty, be cast away in the name of Jesus.

66. I recover my placenta from the cage of wicked people in the name of Jesus.

67. Every agent attached to profitlessness in my life, be paralyzed in the name of Jesus.

68. I receive divine direction in the name of Jesus.

69. O Lord, give me divine revelation in the name of Jesus.

70. O Lord, let your glory overshadow every work that I do, in the name of Jesus.

71. O God, arise and disgrace every trap of poverty in my family, in the name of Jesus.

72. O God, arise and scatter every trap of poverty in my life in the name of Jesus.

73. The labor of my hands shall prosper, in the name of Jesus.

74. Every waster of my prosperity, be rendered impotent, in the name of Jesus.

75. Every known and unknown opposer of my comfort, be paralyzed in the name of Jesus.

76. Anything planted in my life to disgrace me, come out with all your roots in the name of Jesus.

77. I reject demonic stagnation of my blessings in the name of Jesus.
78. I reject weak financial breakthroughs; I claim big financial breakthroughs in the name of Jesus.
79. Every hidden and clever devourer, be bound, in the name of Jesus.
80. I release myself from every family pattern of poverty in the name of Jesus.
81. I refuse to allow my wealth to die on any evil altar, in the name of Jesus.
82. I reject every prosperity paralysis in the name of Jesus.
83. I possess all my foreign benefits today, in the name of Jesus.
84. My pocket will not leak in the name of Jesus.
85. I dash every poverty dream to the ground, in the name of Jesus.
86. Every good thing that my hands have started to build, they shall finish it in the name of Jesus.
87. I refuse to become the foot mat of amputators in the name of Jesus.
88. Let my helpers appear, let my hindrances disappear, in the name of Jesus.
89. God of providence, raised divine capital for me, in the name of Jesus.
90. I occupy my rightful position, in the name of Jesus.
91. Every delayed and denied prosperity, manifest by fire, in the name of Jesus.

92. Every bewitched account, receive deliverance in the name of Jesus.
93. Every snail anointing on my blessings, fall down and die in the name of Jesus.
94. Every power broadcasting my goodness for evil, be silenced in the name of Jesus
95. I refuse to lock the doors of blessings against myself in the name of Jesus.
96. I release myself from every spirit of poverty, in the name of Jesus.
97. I curse the spirit of poverty with the curse of the Lord, in the name of Jesus.
98. I release myself from every bondage of poverty in the name of Jesus.
99. The riches of the gentiles shall come to me.
100. Let divine magnets of prosperity be planted in my hands in the name of Jesus.
101. I retrieve my purse from the hand of Judas, in the name of Jesus.
102. Let there be a reverse transfer of my satanically transferred wealth, in the name of Jesus.
103. I take over the wealth of sinners in the name of Jesus.
104. I recover the steering wheel of my wealth from the hands of evil drivers, in the name of Jesus.
105. O Lord, revive my blessings by fire in the name of Jesus.
106. O Lord, return my stolen blessings unto me a million fold

107. O Lord send out the angels of God to bring me blessings in the name of Jesus.

108. Whatever needs changing in my life to bring me blessings, be changed by fire now in the name of Jesus.

109. Every power sitting on my wealth, fall down and die in the name of Jesus.

110. I shall not be moved, but my mountain shall be moved in the name of Jesus.

111. I shall not give up but my problem shall give up in the name of Jesus.

112. My problem shall surrender in the name of Jesus,

113. I receive the sprinkling of the blood of Jesus into every department of my life in the name of Jesus,

114. I set judgment against every evil altar erected against my destiny in the name of Jesus.

115. O Lord, release my tongue to prosper in the name of Jesus.

116. O Lord, take your place as Lord in my family in the name of Jesus.

117. I receive the power to move my mountains in the name of Jesus.

118. Problems, pack your load and leave my life now in the name of Jesus.

119. Every satanic perfume that covers the glory of God in my life, be wiped off now, in the name of Jesus.

120. Every demonic blanket covering my star, I tear you and destroy you in the name of Jesus.

121. My star must rise and shine clearly in the name of Jesus.
122. My king shall reign in the name of Jesus.
123. O Lord, send out your angels to dig out and destroy every evil root in my life in the name of Jesus.
124. Every wicked weapon fashioned against my life, backfire against the enemy in the name of Jesus.
125. Today, I demand seven fold restitution from satan in the name of Jesus.

Prayer Section

Fourteen

HEALING OF INFIRMITIES

INTRODUCTION

Beloved, you need to be reminded that the salvation our Lord brought to us carried along healing in His wings. In other words, God included His divine healing in His package of salvation for mankind, therefore, it is our right. Despite the unlimited unleash of sicknesses in this present world, the beauty remains that Jesus is still in the business of healing the sick. As long as you are born-again, you are not only entitled to divine healing the power to heal also flows within you. Jesus has paid the price, and He really paid it all, just Isa 53:5 states it *'But he was wounded for our transgressions, he was bruised for our iniquities: the chastisement of our peace was upon him; and with his stripes we are healed.'*

These prayer points are designed to prophesy healing into your life and situation. They will also give you access to that which is yours by right: healing and divine health.

CONFESSION: Malachi 4:2 *'But unto you that fear my name shall the Sun of righteousness arise with healing in his wings; and ye shall go forth, and grow up as calves of the stall.'*

PRAISE WORSHIP

PRAYER POINTS

1. Every kneel of infirmity, in my life, bow, in the name of Jesus.
2. Let the whirlwind scatter every vessel of infirmity fashioned against my life, in the name of Jesus.
3. Let every dead organ in my body, receive life now, in the name of Jesus.
4. Let my blood be transfused with the blood of Jesus to effect perfect health, in the name of Jesus.
5. Let all death contractors assigned against my life begin to kill themselves now, in the name of Jesus.
6. Every infirmity, hiding in any part of my body, come out with all your root, in the name of Jesus.
7. Every spirit, hindering my perfect healing, fall down and die now, in the name of Jesus.
8. I withdraw every conscious and unconscious cooperation with sickness, in the name of Jesus.
9. I release by body from every curse of infirmity, in the name of Jesus.
10. Let the blood of Jesus flush out every evil deposit from my blood, in the name of Jesus.
11. I recover every organ of my body from every evil altar, in the name of Jesus.

12. I annul every engagement with the spirit of death, in the name of Jesus.
13. Father Lord let Your hand of deliverance be stretched out upon my life now, in the name of Jesus.
14. I rebuke every refuge of sickness, in the name of Jesus.
15. I destroy the grip and operation of sickness upon my life, in the name of Jesus.
16. I command death upon any sickness in any area of my life, in the name of Jesus.
17. Let every germ of infirmity in my body die, in the name of Jesus.
18. Let the blood of Jesus flush every evil deposit out from my blood, in the name of Jesus.
19. Every internal disorder, receive order, in the name of Jesus.
20. You messenger of death, come out by fire, in the name of Jesus.
21. Every arrow of death and destruction, go back to your sender, in the name of Jesus.
22. Every spirit, coming to defile my soul and body, i break your backbone today, in the name of Jesus.
23. Lord water me from the waters of God, in the name of Jesus.
24. Every evil thing programmed into my genes, be blotted out by the blood of Jesus, in the name of Jesus.

25. Jesus the great doctor, heal me by your fire today, in the name of Jesus.
26. Healing power of God, come upon me now, in the name of Jesus.
27. My body is not for sickness, in the name of Jesus.
28. Every root of sickness in my life, be uprooted by fire, in the name of Jesus.
29. Every river of affliction in my body, dry up to the root, in the name of Jesus.
30. I command all organs in my body and system to begin to function perfectly, in the name of Jesus.
31. Any of my parents' diseases or infirmity must not locate me, in the name of Jesus.
32. My own case will not be impossible, in the name of Jesus.
33. Begin to thank the Lord for answered prayers.

Prayer Section

Fifteen

CRUSHING THE TEMPLES OF THE DREAM CRIMINALS

INTRODUCTION

Dreams are simply and popularly called spiritual monitors. Your dream is an indicator of what is going on in the spiritual realm. Be informed that many things that happen to you in life had happened in the spiritual; many virtues had been stolen in the dream, many destiny and glory had been caged in the dream, some people's marriages and finances had been concluded right in the dream before their actual manifestation in the physical. Your dream is a monitor of your spiritual life, your physical life has no meaning without your spiritual life thus, whatever happens to your spiritual life manifests in the physical . Therefore, pray these prayers with spirit of no mercy for your enemies and determine to set yourself free today.

CONFESSION: Ps.27:1-2: *'The LORD is my light and my salvation; whom shall I fear? the LORD is the strength of my life; of whom shall I be afraid? When the wicked, even mine enemies and my foes, came upon me to eat up my flesh, they stumbled and fell.'*
1 Cor.10:21: *'Ye cannot drink the cup of the Lord, and the cup of devils: ye cannot be partakers of the Lord's table, and of the table of devils.'*
Ps.91

PRAISE WORSHIP

PRAYER POINTS

1. I claim all the good things which God has revealed to me through dreams. I reject all bad and satanic dreams, in the name of Jesus.
2. (You are going to be specific here. Place your hand on your chest and talk to God specifically about the dreams which need to be cancelled, cancel it with all your strength. If it needs fire, command the fire of God to burn them to ashes in the name of Jesus.)
3. O Lord, perform the necessary surgical operation in my life and change all that had gone wrong in the spirit world, in the name of Jesus.
4. I claim back all the good things which I have lost as a result of defeats and attacks in my dreams, in the name of Jesus.
5. I arrest every spiritual attacker and paralyze their activities in my life, in the name of Jesus.
6. I retrieve my stolen virtues, goodness and blessings, in the name of Jesus.
7. Let all satanic manipulations through dreams be dissolved, in the name of Jesus.
8. Let all arrows, gunshots, wounds, harassment, and opposition in dreams return to the sender, in the name of Jesus.
9. I reject every evil spiritual load placed on me, in the name of Jesus.

10. All spiritual animals (cats, dogs, snakes, crocodiles) paraded against me, be chained and return to your senders, in the name of Jesus.

11. Holy Ghost, purge my intestines and my blood from satanic foods and injections in the name of Jesus.

12. I break every evil covenant and initiation through dreams, in the name of Jesus.

13. I disband all the hosts of darkness set against me, in the name of Jesus.

14. Every evil plan and imagination contrary to my life, fail woefully, in the name of Jesus.

15. Every doorway and ladder to satanic invasion in my life, be abolished forever by the blood of Jesus, in the name of Jesus.

16. I loose myself from curses, hexes, spells, bewitchment and evil domination directed against me through dreams, in the name of Jesus.

17. I command you ungodly powers to release me, in the name of Jesus.

18. Let all past satanic defeats in the dream; be converted to victory, in the name of Jesus.

19. Let all tests in the dream be converted to testimonies, in the name of Jesus.

20. Let all trials in the dream be converted to triumphs, in the name of Jesus.

21. Let all failures in the dream be converted to success, in the name of Jesus.

22. Let all scars in the dream be converted to stars, in the name of Jesus.
23. Let all bondage in the dream be converted to freedom, in the name of Jesus.
24. Let all losses in the dream be converted to gains, in the name of Jesus.
25. Let all opposition in the dream be converted to victory, in the name of Jesus.
26. Let all weaknesses in the dream be converted to strength, in the name of Jesus.
27. Let all negative in the dream; be converted to positive, in the name of Jesus.
28. I release myself from every infirmity introduced into my life through dreams, in the name of Jesus.
29. Let all attempts by the enemy to deceive me through dreams fail woefully, in the name of Jesus.
30. I reject every evil spiritual husband, wife, children, marriage, engagement, trading, pursuit, ornament, money, friend, relatives etc, in the name of Jesus.
31. Lord Jesus, wash my spiritual eyes, ears and mouth with your blood, in the name of Jesus.
32. The God who answereth by fire should answer by fire whenever any spiritual attacker comes against me, in the name of Jesus.
33. Lord Jesus, replace all satanic dreams with heavenly dreams and divinely-inspired dreams in the name of Jesus.

34. I command every evil plantation in my life: come out with all you roots in the name of Jesus. (*Lay your hands on your stomach and keep repeating the emphasized area*)
35. Evil strangers in my body, come out of your hiding place, in the name of Jesus.
36. I disconnect any conscious or unconscious bondage with demonic caterers, in the name of Jesus.
37. Let all the avenues of eating or drinking spiritual poison, be closed, in the name of Jesus.
38. I cough out and vomit any food eaten from the table of the devil, in the name of Jesus. (*Cough them out and vomit them in faith. Prime the expulsion*)
39. Let all negative materials circulating in my bloodstream be evacuated, in the name of Jesus.
40. I drink the blood of Jesus. (*physically drink and swallow it in faith. Keep doing this for some time.*)
41. Let all evil spiritual feeders warring against me eat their own flesh and drink their own blood, in the name of Jesus.
42. I command all demonic food utensils fashioned against me to be roasted, in the name of Jesus.
43. Holy Ghost fire, circulate all over my body, in the name of Jesus.
44. I command all physical poisons within my system to be neutralized, in the name of Jesus.
45. Let all evil assignments fashioned against me through the mouth be nullified, in the name of Jesus.

46. Let all spiritual problems attached to any hour of the night be cancelled, in the name of Jesus. *(Pick the periods from midnight to 6a.m.)*
47. Bread of heaven; fill me till I want no more, in the name of Jesus.
48. Let all catering equipment of evil caterers attached to me be destroyed, in the name of Jesus.
49. I command my digestive system to reject every evil command, in the name of Jesus.
50. Let all satanic designs of oppressions against me in dreams and visions be frustrated, in the name of Jesus.
51. I remove my name from the register of evil feeders with the blood of Jesus, in the name of Jesus.
52. Let the habitation of evil caterers become desolate, in the name of Jesus.
53. I paralyze the spirits that bring bad dreams to me, in the name of Jesus.
54. Let the fire of the Holy Ghost destroy any evil list containing my name, in the name of Jesus.
55. Let the fire of the Holy Ghost destroy any of my photographs in the air, land and sea in the name of Jesus.
56. I destroy any coffin prepared or me, in the name of Jesus.
57. I cancel and wipe off all evil dreams, in the name of Jesus.
58. I destroy every satanic accident organized for my sake, in the name of Jesus.
59. I render all evil night creatures powerless, in the name of Jesus.

60. Let the blood of Jesus wash all organs in my body, in the name of Jesus.
61. Let all sicknesses planted in my body through evil spiritual food be destroyed, in the name of Jesus.
62. Let the blood of Jesus erase all evil dreams in my life, in the name of Jesus.
63. Let the fire of God boil all rivers harboring unfriendly demons, in the name of Jesus.
64. Let all evil dreams be replaced with blessings, in the name of Jesus.
65. I command all my good reams to come to pass, in the name of Jesus.
66. Father Lord, hasten the performance of my good dreams, in the name of Jesus
67. Every spiritual marriage standing against my physical marriage scatter by fire in the name of Jesus.

Prayer Section

Sixteen

BREAKING ANTI-MARRIAGE CURSES AND COVENANTS

INTRODUCTION

In GEN 2:18 the Bible says '*And the LORD God said, It is not good that the man should be alone; I will make him an help meet for him.* A deep look at the creation story shows that after God created everything, the Bible records it that He saw it was good. However, God said it's not good for man to be alone. He therefore created the first institution on earth, marriage, for the man and woman He had created. However, the devil is on rampage and he is fighting against the plan of God. He knows that if two godly Christians meet each and get married, they produce godly children who will wreck great havoc to his kingdom. This is the reason he uses the instruments of curses and covenants to hold people down. These hinder people from marrying the right person, and they are also responsible for late marriage and also attack the finances of people. These prayer points are prepared to destroy these satanic curses and covenants holding down your marital testimony. Pray them with holy anger and the God of Elijah will arise and answer you by fire, in the name of Jesus.

CONFESSION: EPHE6:13-18 '*Wherefore take unto you the whole armour of God, that ye may be able to withstand in the evil day, and having done all, to stand. Stand therefore, having your loins girt about with truth, and having on the breastplate of righteousness; And your feet shod with the*

preparation of the gospel of peace; Above all, taking the shield of faith, wherewith ye shall be able to quench all the fiery darts of the wicked. And take the helmet of salvation, and the sword of the Spirit, which is the word of God: Praying always with all prayer and supplication in the Spirit, and watching thereunto with all perseverance and supplication for all saints;'

PRAISE WORSHIP

PRAYER POINTS

1. Cover yourself with the blood of Jesus and pray thus

    i. Holy Ghost fire, fall on me and burn in my body, soul and spirit, in the name of Jesus.

    ii. Fire of God, go down to my root and burn every evil worm eating up God's plan for my life, in the name of Jesus.

    iii. By the blood of Jesus, I break every evil spiritual marriage vow, in the name of Jesus.

    iv. By the blood of Jesus, I cut myself off from every evil spiritual vow, in the name of Jesus.

    v. In the name of Jesus, I withdraw myself from the evil association of .... (pick from the under listed), in the name of Jesus.

    - The unmarried   - late marriages   - the bewitched
    - God's enemies   - the self-afflicted   - none achievers

2. Every power of the Prince of Persia blocking my prayers all these years, fall down and die, in the name of Jesus.
3. O God of new beginnings, do a new thing in my life in this issue of marriage, and let every eye see it, in the name of Jesus.
4. Strongman man of anti-marriage covenants assigned against my life, roast by fire, in the name of Jesus.
5. Strongman of anti-marriage curses tormenting my life, roast by fire, in the name of Jesus.
6. Servant spirit enforcing anti-marriage covenant in my life, lose your grip over my life and die, in the name of Jesus.
7. Servant spirit, enforcing anti-marriage curses in my life, catch fire and perish, in the name of Jesus.
8. Ancient spiritual marriage of my father's house, claiming ownership over my life, scatter by fire, in the name of Jesus.
9. Ancient spiritual marriage of my mother house, claiming ownership over my life, scatter by fire, in the name of Jesus.
10. I reject and renounce every ancient spirit husband/wife, catch fire and perish, in the name of Jesus.
11. Ancient serpent of spirit husband/wife, assigned to stop my godly marriage, stretch, catch fire and burn to ashes, in the name of Jesus.
12. Anti-marriage covenant, holding down my life in captivity, break, in the name of Jesus.
13. Anti-marriage curses keeping me in bondage, break and scatter, in the name of Jesus.

14. O God arise and deliver me from the slavery of spiritual marriage, in the name of Jesus.
15. Marriage opportunities that I have lost as a result of anti-marital curses and covenants, I recover you back by fire, in the name of Jesus.
16. Any witch or wizard that that has been married to me in the spirit, using my marital glory to prosper, you shall die, in the name of Jesus.
17. Anti-marriage and soul tie covenant keeping me in the same level, break, in the name of Jesus.
18. Every anti-marriage yoke, holding me in captivity, be destroedy by the power of the HolyGhost, in the name of Jesus.
19. I come out of the evil pattern assigned to me by anti-marriage curses and covenant, in the name of Jesus.
20. By the blood of Jesus and the mercy of God, O God arise and propel me into my godly marriage, in the name of Jesus.
21. Anything in my life, that is reinforcing anti-marriage curses and covenant, die, in the name of Jesus.
22. Evil cloud of anti-marriage curses and covenants, hiding me away from my godly spouse, clear away by fire, in the name of Jesus.
23. O God arise and perfect everything that concerns my godly marriage, in the name of Jesus.
24. Every inherited marital curse waging war against my life, break by fire, in the name of Jesus.

25. I speak woe upon any satanic altar issuing curses against my marital breakthrough, in the name of Jesus.
26. Every covenant of darkness saying I will marry wrongly, what are you waiting for, break, in the name of Jesus.
27. Any power pouring libation on the earth against my marital testimony, somersault and die, in the name of Jesus.
28. Every yoke of darkness upon my marital breakthrough, break by fire, in the name of Jesus.
29. I destroy by fire, any power of my father's house, polluting my marital breakthrough, in the name of Jesus.
30. Every curse issued by my parents against my marital testimony, break, in the name of Jesus.
31. Every curse of darkness issued by my relatives, I break you, in the name of Jesus.
32. Any satanic covenant with the earth holding unto my marital breakthrough, break by fire, in the name of Jesus.
33. Every satanic gathering issuing woes upon my marital breakthrough, die, in the name of Jesus.
34. Strongman of darkness in my locality driving away my divine spouse, fall and die, in the name of Jesus.
35. Any satanic animal, eating my marital testimony, die by fire, in the name of Jesus.
36. O God arise and destroy every satanic stronghold upon my marital testimony, in the name of Jesus.

37. I challenge any power that has vowed not to let me go with the fire of the Holy Ghost, in the name of Jesus.
38. Every power waiting for my day of testimony in order to attack me, somersault and die, in the name of Jesus.
39. O God arise and deliver me with a mighty and outstretched arm from powers too strong for me, in the name of Jesus.
40. Every satanic coven, holding me down maritally, break by fire, in the name of Jesus.
41. Spiritual marriage to my ancestors, holding my marriage, break, in the name of Jesus.
42. Spiritual marriage to my parents, be destroyed, in the name of Jesus.
43. Spiritual marriage to the dead, stopping my physical marriage from manifesting, break, in the name of Jesus.
44. Blood of Jesus, arrow of God's deliverance, deliver me now from.....(pick from the under listed), in the name of Jesus.

    - spirit of late marriage   - spirit of error
    - spirit of disappointment - spirit of loneliness
45. Strange marks on my life, be robbed off by the blood of Jesus, in the name of Jesus.
46. Any satanic wedding suit/gown upon my life, roast by fire, in the name of Jesus.
47. Marriage with the spirits of the water, break, in the name of Jesus.
48. Marriage with forest spirits, be destroyed, in the name of

49. I decree total desolation upon the habitation of the stubborn strongman, in the name of Jesus.

50. Every unconscious covenant, chasing away my divine spouse, break by fire, in the name of Jesus.

51. Divine boldness, come upon my divine spouse, in the name of Jesus.

52. Any power mocking my prayers, your time is up, die, in the name of Jesus.

53. I shall laugh last, in the name of Jesus.

54. Any power that wants to attack me as a result of these prayers, your time is up, die, in the name of Jesus.

55. Angels of the living God, search the land of the living and the land of the dead, and gather all fragmented parts of my life together, in the name of Jesus.

56. I break every barrier between me and my divine spouse, in the name of Jesus.

57. Right now, O Lord, let Your sword of deliverance touch my blood, in the name of Jesus.

58. O Lord, open Your book of remembrance for me now, in the name of Jesus.

59. Thank the Lord for answers to your prayers.

Prayer Section

Seventeen

DOMINION PRAYERS

INTRODUCTION
This particular section of prayer is meant to usher you into your dominion; take it with strong faith and let the level of your determination be increased for an over-whelming result. May God perfect your joy, in the mighty name of Jesus.

CONFESSION: psalm 34:10 *'The young lions do lack, and suffer hunger: but they that seek the LORD shall not want any good thing.*
Psalm 113:5, 7, 8 *'Who is like unto the LORD our God, who dwelleth on high, He raiseth up the poor out of the dust, and lifteth the needy out of the dunghill;That he may set him with princes, even with the princes of his people.*

PRAISE WORSHIP

PRAYER POINTS

1. Thank God for His provision so far.
2. Let all security man in charge of satanic banks that are harbouring my blessings, be paralysed, in the name of Jesus.
3. I terminate the appointment of all satanic bankers and managers, in the name of Jesus.

4. I command the thunder of God to break to pieces all the satanic strong-rooms harbouring by properties, in the name of Jesus.
5. I possess all my properties, in the name of Jesus.
6. Let all satanic instruments (the legal tenders and the cheque) used against me be completely destroyed, in the name of Jesus.
7. I command all satanic clearing houses and agents to be roasted, in the name of Jesus.
8. I paralyse completely all satanic transactions and contracts against my life, in the name of Jesus.
9. Let all satanic networks and computers fashioned against me be disorganized, in the name of Jesus.
10. Heavenly Father, let all the blood that has been stored up in any satanic bank come forth, in the name of Jesus.
11. I refuse to be an object for satanic transaction, in the name of Jesus.
12. I refuse to do profitless work, in the name of Jesus.
13. Every evil force, against my handiwork, be paralysed, in the name of Jesus.
14. I send back to the sender, every arrow of spiritual deposit and advanced payment against my handiwork, in the name of Jesus.
15. You my handiwork, receive divine profit, in the name of Jesus.
16. I cover my handiwork with the fire of God, in the name of Jesus.

17. I cover my handiwork with hot coals of fire, untouchable for evil forces, in the name of Jesus.

18. Lord put to shame, every evil force that is against my handiwork, in the name of Jesus.

19. My handiwork, receive the touch of the Lord, in the name of Jesus.

20. Every tree of profitless hard-work be uprooted, in the name of Jesus.

21. Lord bring me into favour with all those that will decide on my advancement, in the name of Jesus.

22. Lord cause a divine substitution to happen, if this is what will move me ahead, in the name of Jesus.

23. I reject the spirit of the tail, and I claim the spirit of the head, in the name of Jesus.

24. I command all evil records planted by the devil in any one's mind against my advancement to be shattered to pieces, in the name of Jesus.

25. Lord transfer, remove, or change all human agents that are bent on stopping my advancement, in the name of Jesus.

26. Lord smoothen out my path to the top by the hand of fire, in the name of Jesus.

27. I receive the anointing to excel above my contemporaries, in the name of Jesus.

28. Lord, catapult me to greatness as you did for Daniel in the land of Babylon, in the name of Jesus.

29. Lord, help me identify and deal with any weaknesses in me that can hinder my progress, in the name of Jesus.
30. I bind every strongman dedicated to hinder my progress, in the name of Jesus.
31. Lord dispatch your angels to roll away every stumbling block to my promotion, advancement and elevation, in the name of Jesus.
32. I receive the mandate to put to flight, every enemy of my breakthroughs, in the name of Jesus.
33. Let the mark of the blood of Jesus, of divine favour and protection be upon my life, in the name of Jesus.
34. Lord prepare me as a living sanctuary for you, in the name of Jesus.
35. Father Lord, rent the heavens and come down at my cry, in the name of Jesus.
36. Let every terrestrial and celestial spirit working against me be paralysed, in the name of Jesus.
37. Let power from above, fall on me to do the impossible, in the name of Jesus.
38. Let every good and perfect gift locate me today, in the name of Jesus.
39. I prophesy unto every imperfect gift in my life to become perfect, in the name of Jesus.
40. I command the rain of abundance, goodness, favour and mercy to fall on every department of my life, in the name of Jesus.
41. Let divine glory from above overshadow my life now, in the name of Jesus.
42. I paralyse every enemy that is against my open heavens, in the name of Jesus.
43. I paralyse all powers that expand problems, in the name of Jesus.

44. I paralyse all powers that delay miracles, in the name of Jesus.
45. I paralyse all marriage destroyers, in the name of Jesus.
46. I paralyse all anti-marriage agents, in every area of my life, in the name of Jesus.
47. Lord make me a channel of your blessings in all areas of life, in the name of Jesus.
48. Let my hands be stronger than all opposing hands, in the name of Jesus.
49. Every stone of hindrance, be rolled out of my way, in the name of Jesus.
50. My tongue become an instrument of God's glory, in the name of Jesus.
51. I command every satanic embargo on my goodness and prosperity to be scattered to irreparable pieces, in the name of Jesus.
52. Let every door of attack on my progress be closed, in the name of Jesus.
53. I command all my imprisoned benefits to be released, in the name of Jesus.
54. O Lord anoint me to pull down the negative stronghold strongholds manufactured against me, in the name of Jesus.
55. I receive the anointing and possess the power to pursue, overtake and recover my stolen blessings, in the name of Jesus.
56. The enemy shall not have a hiding place in my life, in the name of Jesus.
57. I enter into my realm of dominion, in the name of Jesus.

Made in the USA
Columbia, SC
12 May 2021

37737278R00089

Made in the USA
Monee, IL
21 November 2021

82440965R00046